The New Prince

ALSO BY DICK MORRIS

Bum Rap on America's Cities:
The Real Cause of Urban Decay

Behind the Oval Office:
Getting Reelected Against All Odds

The New Prince

MACHIAVELLI UPDATED FOR THE TWENTY-FIRST CENTURY

DICK MORRIS

RENAISSANCE BOOKS

Los Angeles

Copyright © 1999 by Dick Morris

All rights reserved. Reproduction without permission in writing from the publisher is prohibited, except for brief passages in connection with a review. For
permission, write: Renaissance Books, 5858 Wilshire Boulevard, Suite 200, Los
Angeles, California 90036.

Library of Congress Cataloging-in-Publication Data
Morris, Dick.
    The new prince / Dick Morris.
        p. cm.
    ISBN 1-58063-079-0 (alk. paper)
    1. Politics, Practical—United States. 2. Political leadership—
United States. 3. United States—Politics and government.
I. Title.
JK1726.M65 1999
324.7'0973'09045—dc21   99-21767
                                                              CIP

10 9 8 7 6 5 4 3 2 1

Design by Lisa-Theresa Lenthall
Typesetting by James Tran

Distributed by St. Martin's Press
Manufactured in the United States of America

First Edition

To my mother, Terry Morris, for her idealism. To my father, Eugene J. Morris, for his pragmatism. To my wife, Eileen McGann, for her embrace of both.

Acknowledgments

I have found a publisher to love in Renaissance Books. May we grow old together. Arthur Morey is a skilled editor who leaves his superego at home. Bill Hartley is a man who sees the possible and makes it the probable. Mike Dougherty impresses even me with his public relations skills. Mike Levine introduced me to this crew and made it all happen. And can Lisa Lenthall design a cover or what?

Contents

PART 3
GETTING ELECTED

E P I L O G U E
T H E   F U T U R E

Preface

This book is based on a single premise: If American politicians were truly pragmatic and did what was really in their own best self-interest, our political process would be a lot more clean, positive, nonpartisan, and issue-oriented. It is not practicality which drives the partisanship, negativity, and the never-ending cycle of investigation and recrimination in which we wallow, but a complete misapprehension of what Americans want and what politicians—in their own career self-interest—should offer. If Machiavelli were alive today, he would counsel idealism as the most pragmatic course.

Pragmatism has gotten a bad name; Machiavellianism is in even lower repute. They have become synonymous with skulduggery, manipulation, and deceit. But the mandate of the pragmatist in a democracy is not to descend to the lowest possible level. It is simply to be practical—to do the best job he can of winning elections and maintaining popular support for his program after he is elected.

As the American people change, pragmatists must change with them. In the past few decades, voters have become vastly better informed, more centrist, more sophisticated, and increasingly disgusted with the negative tone of our politics. But politicians and the news media don't get it. Politicians only dish out and the media only cover the most negative, simplistic, distorted, and partisan rhetoric possible. Too often our elections are a race to the bottom—a contest to see who can sink the lowest. This is not just bad government, it's stupid politics.

The tasks of winning office and of governing are far harder now than they have ever been. The aggressiveness of the media and the virtual suspension of all rules of decency in political combat have made getting elected and serving in office successfully almost insuperable challenges. Once, parties contested with each other only during election periods; today they fight each day, and offer neither quarter nor respite.

This book is a practical guide for anyone who must deal with the political process in any way. It is for the politician who wants to win office, hold it, and pass his program. But its lessons are no less important for the staffs, advisors, and consultants to these men and women; those who lobby and advocate issues will also find the insights relevant. Hopefully, this book will not appeal just to political players, but to the voters as well. A knowledge of the techniques, intricacies, and evolution of the practical politics of our era will help create a better and more selective electorate.

The core advice of this book is to stay positive; to focus on the issues; to rise above party; and to lead through ideas. This is not idealism. It is pragmatism in America today. Our candidates and office holders need to change their tactics, their focus, and their strategies—not in the interest of better government, but in order to succeed in their chosen line of work.

I disagree with the current bulk of the conventional wisdom about politics. In the Part 1 overview, I take issue with the flawed view of most political analysts who overstate the power of money, spin, scandal, voter self-interest, and image. Message is more important than money. Issues are more central than image. Strategy matters more than tactics. Positives work better than negatives. Substance is more salient than scandal. Issues are more powerful than image, and strategy more important than spin. The more partisan you are, the less effective you will be. Appeals rooted in generosity and the public interest do better than those which appeal to the voters' self-interest. Voters want to hear about how to make their lives better, not richer. Values matter more than economics.

In Part 2, I apply these ideas to the daily process of governing. In the spirit of the original Prince, I try to help an incumbent president, governor, senator, congressman, state legislator, or councilman succeed in the modern political world.

In Part 3, I go back to the beginning and speak directly to candidates and their staffs, walking them through the process of getting elected and reelected.

Lest this book appear to be an advertisement for my services as a political consultant, I have left that part of my life behind and no longer work in American elections.

My goal in writing *The New Prince* is to identify what the modern pragmatist must do to win. He or she must possess far more idealism than is currently seen in American political figures. Those who want to win in America today had better adjust their attitudes, strategies, and tactics upward.

And only the Master shall praise us; only the Master shall blame
And no one shall work for money; and no one shall work for fame.
But each for the joy of working; each by his own special star
Shall draw the thing as he sees it, for the God of things as they are!
—Rudyard Kipling

PART 1

The Pragmatism of Idealism

When the earth moves, it's time to redraw the map. The enormous shifts and changes in voter attitudes during the past twenty years have so changed our politics that it is time to reexamine each assumption and scrutinize the axioms on which practical politics are based.

The central shift is from a paradigm of representative democracy, where voters cede their power every two years to their elected representatives, to one where direct citizen involvement and interest is almost constant. This transition from Madisonian to Jeffersonian norms is so dramatic and drastic that it forces a reevaluation of all our traditional notions of politics.

In modern politics, a candidate's positive issue message, the substance of his candidacy, has become far more important than money, image, spin, negative attacks, and political party. In the service of pragmatism, not of idealism, we must become more idealistic.

CHAPTER 1

The Transition from Madisonian to Jeffersonian Democracy

THE FUNDAMENTAL PARADIGM that dominates our politics is the shift from representational (Madisonian) to direct (Jeffersonian) democracy. Voters want to run the show directly and are impatient with all forms of intermediaries between their opinions and public policy. This basic shift stems from a profusion of information on the one hand, and a determined distrust of institutions and politicians on the other.

While the media has noted decreasing voter turnout, the corollary is that those who do vote are becoming better and better informed. Americans are now an electorate of information junkies. Through the CNN, Fox News Channel, CNBC, CFN, MSNBC, and C-SPAN TV networks, talk radio, all-news radio, news magazines, the Internet, prime-time TV shows like *60 Minutes* and *20/20*, and the nightly news on the major TV networks, voters are fed an overwhelming diet of information about the political process. Even entertainment shows focus on public-sector issues, as the cops-and-robbers programs explore the subtleties of the exclusionary rule and attorney-client privilege. Taxi drivers who watch congressional hearings on C-SPAN are better informed about public policy than they have ever been.

With this level of information has come a certitude about political opinions. Where once voters were inclined to subordinate their own views to those of wiser heads, they now feel capable of analyzing public-policy issues themselves. In the 1960s, it was common to hear people say that their leaders had access to more information, that it was wrong to judge them without knowing all the facts. Now, we would laugh at anyone who said that on television.

Impatient with representative assemblies, voters take lawmaking into their own hands when the politicians let them. For example, ever since referenda became popular in California, the state legislature has increasingly become a ministerial body, executing the broad policy decisions made by voters themselves, through the ten or twelve ballot issues they decide each election day.

As the electorate has become more opinionated and self-confident, its distrust of politicians, parties, and all institutions has become more profound. Watergate was the original scandal of modern American political life. But since then, each institution has had its own scandal: doctors have had malpractice scandals; evangelicals have had the Bakker and Swaggert scandals; the intelligence community has had the Aldrich Ames scandal; journalists have had plagiarism scandals; labor unions have had corruption and mob scandals; lawyers have had malpractice scandals; churches have had child sex-abuse scandals; the military has had the Pentagon procurement scandals; police departments have had local corruption scandals and the Rodney King beating. No institution remains unscathed. Voters trust themselves . . . and nobody else.

This underlying shift in our electorate's mood, away from blind faith and toward self-reliance, is combining with a new technology which empowers voters as never before. Political polling now rates politicians every day of their term and broadcasts the findings for all to see. Referenda, initiatives, and even recalls of elected officials increasingly dominate policy-making. The proliferation of TV channels and the growth of talk radio offer forums for political debate never before available in such length or depth. Soon, interactive TV-computers will allow national town meetings with direct balloting by tens of millions of people—the very core of the Jeffersonian vision of small-town democracy at work.

One by-product of this shift in power from politicians to voters is the decline of ideology. Voters want to think for themselves and will not buy the prefabricated, predictable opinions of either left- or right-wing ideologues. Men of affairs who respond to each new situation with practical, specific ideas unfettered by ideological constructs increasingly dominate our political process.

Felix Rohayten described the difference between French and American politics when he said, "The French respect ideas over facts. Americans respect facts over ideas."

Once, American voters didn't really have access to the facts. News information was sharply limited and controlled by the three networks. Without an impressive array of facts at their disposal, voters had no choice but to rely on ideologies or "ideas." It was easier to learn one point of view which provided a formula for analysis of all issues than it was to gather data about each question and think it through on its own merits.

But now that the information is practically force-fed to the voters, ideology becomes an unnecessary guide. Rather than try to fit the facts into preconceived opinions, voters would rather change their preconceptions as they learn new facts. As Winston Churchill once told a woman who criticized him for changing his position on an issue: "When the facts change, I change my opinions. What is it, madam, that you do?" Ideas, the preconceived formulas of the ideologies, matter less to Americans than do the facts of each specific situation. Voters want what works, no matter whose ideological label it bears.

Americans are more and more independent politically. A plurality—40 percent of the electorate—now does not profess allegiance to either political party or vote a party line. Increasingly unwilling to trust Democrats or Republicans, they believe that the executive branch and the Congress should be controlled by different political parties. These independent voters do not care about party labels. They insist on examining each candidate on his or her own merits, irrespective of party. Even when the public opinion shifts support from one party to another, it is voters who were once loyal to one of the parties who switch to the other. Independents remain independent.

The trend from Madisonian to Jeffersonian governance is changing all the rules. Few realize how fundamentally the rules have changed. In most cases, a pessimism stops them from celebrating the transformation which is underway. In the next ten chapters, we will explore how this transition to direct democracy is changing everything.

The right wing liked to say, years ago, that America was a republic, not a democracy. Now it is a democracy.

CHAPTER 2

Message over Money

F ORMER SPEAKER OF THE HOUSE Tip O'Neill said that money is "the mother's milk of politics." When he said it, he was right. Now he's wrong. Money in politics is not nearly as important as everybody thinks it is. Message is vastly more important. Candidates need sufficient funds to carry their case to the voters, but financial superiority is not crucial. More money helps. But its importance is universally overrated. A richer candidate with a weaker message will generally lose to a poorer candidate with a stronger message as long as the candidate with more limited money has enough funds to get his or her message out.

Consider the epitaphs in the graveyard of failed but well-funded candidacies: Perot for president, Forbes for president, Huffington for senator in California, Stein and Lauder for mayor in New York City, Bredeson for governor in Tennessee, Milner for governor in Georgia, Williams for governor in Texas, Romney for senator in Massachusetts, Lehrman for governor in New York State, Shavonni for senator in Connecticut, Eckert for governor in Florida, and Short for senator in Minnesota. Each marks a candidate who lost despite having virtually unlimited money. They died with their boots on and their wallets depleted. Of the twenty-four victorious candidates I have handled in races for senator or governor, thirteen had less money than their opponents. Some had a lot less. Even though Bob Dole outspent Bill Clinton in 1996 by 2-to-1, he still lost.

The increasing importance of message over money is part of the shift from representative to direct democracy. In a representative democracy, voters worry deeply about what kind of man or woman will represent them in Congress or as governor. They carefully weigh character in evaluating whom to trust with their vote. But as voters become more certain of their own opinions, they worry less about to whom they will delegate their power, and more about whether or not their representative will echo their own points of view. Thus, character counts for less and message counts for more.

If anyone doubts this proposition, we have only to examine the continuing popularity of Bill Clinton in the face of the Lewinsky scandal. With the right message, the character and image of the candidate is a lot less important.

Message is much cheaper to project than character. To get someone to agree with you costs less than to try to get him to like you. As a candidate's views and ideas come to matter more than his personality or character, campaigns cost less. While the typical wealthy candidate is hiring top image-makers to design gorgeous ads showing his roots in the soil and his family values, the poorer candidate is running ads about issues—and overcoming the financial disadvantage by having something to say.

To win, a candidate does not need the kind of money most politicians, media, fund-raisers, and donors think is necessary. The key to running a campaign on the cheap is to avoid spending money on anything other than projecting a message. Rich candidates squander millions on headquarters, staff, duplicative consultants, and the like. A candidate needs enough money to get his or her message across.

How much is enough?

In a typical television advertising campaign, it takes about one thousand gross rating points (GRPs) to pound a message home. One GRP means that 1 percent of the households in a media market are watching your ad. One thousand GRPs means that most voters see your ad about seven to nine times during the campaign, and some see it much more frequently.

The cost-per-GRP ranges widely depending on the size of the market and on whether or not the ad is to run in prime time. In New York City, where media costs an average of $600 per GRP for a political candidate for a thirty-second ad, it would cost about $600,000 to punch a message through. In Jackson, Mississippi, where it costs $25 per GRP, you'd need only $25,000. In the average media market in a medium-sized city, it costs about $125 per GRP, or about $125,000, to get a single message across. In a statewide race, with many different media markets, the cost will be proportionately more.

A successful candidate usually needs to project eight to ten messages per campaign. That's eight to ten thousand GRPs or, in a typical media market, a total price tag of $800,000 to $1 million. In a midsize typical state, the price tag will run to about $2.5 million.

That's what "enough" is.

Exorbitant? Not in the real world. Any serious contender for senator or governor in a typical state should be able to raise this sum. To raise $2.5 million, you need 1,250 families to give $2,000 each. While this may be a prohibitive cost for a fringe candidate, it is well within the capacity of almost any viable contender.

Republicans, in particular, overestimate the impact of money on politics. Often GOP political strategy seems like the human-wave theory of the Chinese military translated to politics. Where Beijing uses masses of soldiers to overwhelm their adversaries, the GOP uses huge campaign budgets as a substitute for strategy, thought, or issues. But just as technology and advanced weaponry can defeat the Red Army, so enough money, spent on the right message, will defeat gigantic campaign spending.

In their mad pursuit of funds, many candidates foolishly ignore the need to develop a good message. They don't spend the hours they need thinking about what all this money will be spent to say. Millionaires run for office expecting to buy their way to victory without the least thought for the content of their campaigns. Sometimes pure financial advantage works, as it did for Heinz in Pennsylvania, Lautenberg in New Jersey, Bennett in Utah, and Brown in Kentucky. But the failures are far more common.

The arrogant failure to think out a message is the concomitant of campaigns that stress image over substance. In both cases, the politician is hoping to win by manipulation rather than by persuasion. But both approaches ignore rapidly increasing educational levels and galloping informational levels, among the American voters. The American electorate will accept only substance, not glitz, as a campaign message.

Candidates often focus on matching or exceeding the money their adversaries have raised, rather than pausing to calculate rationally how much it costs to get a message across. For all the obsessive focus on fund-raising in American politics today, it is the supreme irony that much of the time politicians spend raising money is wasted because they have not thought out the message they want that money to bring to the voters. Like bidders at an auction, they vie for the lead in fund-raising and seek sums that are out of all proportion to what is really required to win. Of such delusions are the sweet dreams of political consultants made.

Politics is not a mechanical process; it is dominated by ideas. Money doesn't talk. Indeed, without a message, it has nothing to say.

CHAPTER 3

Issues over Image

IMAGE REIGNS SUPREME in our politics. It shouldn't. Media experts rely too heavily on thematic, emotional, or visual appeals in political campaigning. Shaped by the norms of commercial advertising, where the image is all, they fall in love with their own cameras as they try to capture—or, when necessary, create—their candidate's personality on film. They make Bill Clinton look young and vibrant; President Bush, grandfatherly and kind; Reagan, avuncular and empathetic.

But the basic premise of image campaigns is outdated. Elections used to be the time to decide who will make the decisions for our government, to whom the voters should delegate their power. But the modern electorate doesn't want to cede its direct role in determining policy to any party or anyone.

One of the reasons politicians like Clinton have proven less vulnerable than one might expect to constant attacks on their characters, is that voters don't want to have to trust a candidate to make decisions for them. They want their elected officials on a shorter leash. Voters now insist that a candidate spell out his program, his vision, his ideas, and then they will elect him to fulfill that specific mandate. As Tina Turner sang, "What's love got to do with it?"

In our age of direct Jeffersonian democracy, the surest way to capture a voter is to educate him. Just as programs like *60 Minutes* or *20/20* do well in ratings because they entertain by informing, so campaigns do best when their ideas move the electorate's thinking one step ahead. Campaigns are the time to help the electorate grow intellectually; the candidates whose media message catalyzes that process will win the voters' strong support.

Image advertisements pushing "feel-good" themes don't create lasting voter support. At most, they can carry momentum after issues have generated it.

Voters are well aware that the young men and women who carry storyboards through the carpeted corridors of advertising agencies have the creative ability to seduce them with images and appearances. The Darwinian adaptive trait of our time is the ability to figure out when we are being lied to on television. Lest we change beer brands with each new ad or buy a different car each month, we have learned since birth to view all advertising with the greatest of skepticism.

Image ads may satiate a focus group for a few hours, but they don't do well over the long campaign. Voters demand specifics and want content. Image ads too often resemble bank commercials—long on style and short on substance—because there is too little real difference in the products being offered. Elections are won by verbs—proposals for action—not by adjectives which flatter a candidate.

Sometimes the power of issues is obvious, as when a great question like abortion, the Vietnam War, Watergate, or Social Security has such power that, by itself, it moves voters; then it really doesn't matter who's running. Voters in effect treat the election as a ballot referendum on a gut-wrenching issue. The author of the best set of issue positions wins, whether he has acne or not.

Not only are issue messages more effective than image ads in getting votes, they are even better able to explain the true character and personality of the candidate. America's skeptical and well-informed electorate distrusts any other way of judging candidates. Anyone can create an ad full of adjectives or fancy production values. We have learned from Gary Hart, Dan Quayle, and others not to believe our own eyes. When a political ad shows us youth and charisma, it might just be a Robert Redford look-alike in a real-life version of the film *The Candidate*. Biographic ads showcasing "achievements" are only slightly more credible. We have heard awful scoundrels claim credit for accomplishments that lie beyond the horizons of human imagination. When a candidate says, for example, that he "created" hundreds of thousands of jobs, it strains credibility with a public that knows full well that the Federal Reserve Board, the president, the Congress, and the business cycle itself might also have had something to do with it.

But when a candidate takes an issue position in the thick of controversy, voters feel that is the most reliable indicator they have of his true essence. Voters know he has chosen sides. They know the controversial position will make him enemies and alienate interest groups. The issue position becomes a form of symbolic speech, telling us what the candidate is all about. A candidate's issue positioning may not be much, but it's all we have.

For example, Clinton's support of college scholarships had salience beyond its appeal to college students and parents. It illustrated his commitment to opportunity, compassion about poverty, and faith in learning. The Medicare issue in 1995–1996 reached the young as well as the elderly since it spoke of Clinton's caring and values, and painted those who backed major cuts as callous and indifferent.

Clinton learned the importance of issues in 1980 when he became "America's youngest former governor," a distinction of which he soon tired. In his defeat in 1980, Clinton hired a former furniture dealer-turned-media creator, who used beautiful cinematography to produce glorious tributes to Clinton's youth, energy, and charisma, and to capture the emotion of a state on the move. Meanwhile, Clinton's Republican adversary, Frank White, hammered him ungenerously for raising car licensing fees and for letting Cuban refugees stay in Arkansas where President Carter had stashed them. White's issue ads overwhelmed Clinton's feel-good media. Inferring image from issues, voters felt Clinton's insensitivity in raising fees and coddling refugees showed that his Yale education had overshadowed his Arkansas roots.

In his 1982 comeback, Clinton used issues, not image, to defeat Frank White. Urging direct election of the Public Utilities Commission, he attacked high electric bills, showing his populism and empathy. Upon recapturing the governorship, he demanded that teachers pass competency tests to keep their jobs. Through this highly controversial proposal, he showed his concern for children and his independence of teachers' unions. He realized that he could never use images or adjectives to bring his message to Arkansas; he needed issues to drive it home.

After a time—a long time—a political figure's issues will congeal into a permanent image. After trying to limit Medicare spending for most of 1995, former Speaker Newt Gingrich finally earned the adjectives "harsh" and "cruel," while Clinton's nightly defense of the program made him seem "reasonable" and "caring." Truman's bashing of the Republican Congress showed him to be "feisty." Kennedy's embrace of civil rights helped this most cautious man to seem "courageous." Johnson's prevarications over Vietnam left him with an image as being "untruthful." But the adjectives followed the positioning, not the other way around.

In our memory, we remember the politician's attributes, the adjectives we used to describe them. We celebrate Clinton's compassion and deplore Gingrich's insensitivity. But our recollection is playing tricks on us. We remember the adjectives, but we forget the issues that fixed them in our minds. Long after the issue has disappeared from view, the adjective remains, the residue of the issue.

So voters learn who their candidates are through issues. The issues then suggest adjectives and attributes. These ideas about their personality and character fix themselves in our minds. Then we forget about the issues and remember only the characteristics. But the key is to use the issues to trigger the adjectives.

CHAPTER 4

Positives over Negatives

V OTERS HATE NEGATIVE ADS. They have always hated them. But they used to work better than any other type of ad, so candidates used them. Now they don't. Still, candidates rely on them—often to their detriment.

As the public's mood has changed and its sophistication has grown, positives and negatives have alternated in their control of the political battlefield. In the 1960s, America was in love with her politicians. Still dazzled by the Kennedy charisma, positive ads worked well and tended to dominate elections. With the Vietnam/Watergate/Energy crises of the 1970s, the good mood faded and negatives had the advantage. A politician hit with a negative had the burden of proof to establish his innocence in front of a cynical electorate.

But the pendulum has swung back. People have become jaded by negative ads. More optimistic and positive toward government than they were in the 1970s and early 1980s, voters have begun to become deeply suspicious of negative media.

Part of this skepticism about negative messages comes from our greater sophistication and understanding of personality. The rigid morality that doomed Gary Hart has given way to the maturity and depth of perspective which leads to forgiveness of Bill Clinton. People understand that a spot on one's record or a blemish on a politician's character is not necessarily a disqualification that affects all other aspects of a candidate's personality.

Similarly, voters are much more wary of negative information about a candidate's issue positions. The vast amount of information and data poured on them over television and radio each day has made them more savvy in assessing attacks against a politician's voting record.

Once, voters would have summarily rejected a politician who was accused of backing "cuts" in Social Security. Now our better-educated electorate is likely to ask if the vote was indeed for "cuts" in benefits, or only for adjustments in the way cost-of-living increases for Social Security are calculated to reflect more current inflation data. Knowing the growing strains on the Social Security system, a negative ad on Social Security might backfire if the candidate under attack could show that his vote had actually helped to stabilize the system and protect it for the future.

For negatives to work, they usually have to rely on a simplistic, knee-jerk reaction from voters that can be brought to a fever pitch in thirty seconds. But voters' greater subtlety in understanding both the variables of personality and the intricacies of issues make negatives a harder sell than ever before.

If negative ads don't work, they have an increasing potential to blow up in the face of the candidate who sponsored them. The rule these days is, *He who asserts, must prove.* When a negative ad fails to live up to this substantial burden, or is destroyed by a rebuttal ad, the campaign that threw the negative endangers its own credibility. Rebut the negative, and the opposing campaign has not merely lost a skirmish, it has suffered almost irreparable damage. An effective rebuttal makes it hard for the campaign whose negative ad is destroyed to be believed about anything ever again.

Obviously, if a candidate stands quietly by and absorbs punishment like Mike Dukakis did in 1988, negatives work. But rebuttals can protect most candidates against the destructive power of negatives.

Campaigns cannot win if they are based on a negative message. Negatives have their place, but they do not form the essential structure of a winning campaign. They are sometimes used as tactical tools to gain an advantage. But most of the time, negatives will only work once you've laid out a raison d'être for your candidacy through positive ads.

Campaigns start with competing messages. The key to winning any race is to come up with an affirmative message that outdistances your opponents' message. It is the inability to understand this simple, straightforward point that causes more losses in politics than any other single factor. Neither a financial advantage, nor a better negative campaign, nor a superior field organization matters nearly as much as getting the right affirmative message established at the start of a race.

Usually, one can rebut the normal "you voted this way and I voted that way" negatives. So many votes are cast in Congress that almost every senator or congressman has cast votes that seem to prove almost anything. It is very hard to make a negative stick in the face of a proper rebuttal ad.

The two positive messages of opposing sides of a campaign cruise alongside each other like the naval fleets of old, each seeking to get the lead. Better conceived, more resonant, and salient, one message begins to pull ahead. Eventually it gains so much momentum that it leaves the opponent with no option but to throw negatives to catch up. Off balance, failing and flailing, the losing side turns nasty. But in today's politics, negatives do not triumph unless the candidate under fire has either run off with the cookie jar or fails to answer the attack.

When one campaign outdistances the other, pulling ahead with its positive message, forcing the other side into negatives, the winning side in effect performs the classic naval maneuver of crossing the T—cutting in front of the other fleet, showing its broadside to the hapless, oncoming vessels. If the winning campaign trains its rebuttal—its broadside—on the oncoming negative ads, destroying each desperate negative attack, victory is inevitable. As the losing candidate fires negatives, the winner can volley back with rebuttals that administer the coup de grace by destroying the credibility of the attacking campaign.

In articulating the affirmative message of a campaign, comparisons between the issue positions may be necessary. If these comparisons are just thin disguises for negatives, voters will catch on quickly. If the comparisons of the issue positions are accurate and reflect the real opinions of the candidates, they may work. But a comparison ad will work best if the affirmative issue message strikes home.

In the 1996 campaign, Clinton's early advertising and issue positioning closed the Republican lead and opened up a decisive Democratic margin instead. Then as the campaign progressed, the Clinton campaign forces shifted to the defensive, in effect inviting the Dole campaign to attack. As with the metaphor of naval combat, Clinton had crossed Dole's "T." Having outdistanced Dole through positive issue positioning and substantive comparisons, the Democratic campaign got into position and awaited the Republican negatives. When Dole's attacks came, Clinton was ready with devastating broadsides. Deliberately sitting on the defensive, the Clinton campaign returned each negative blast with a scorching rebuttal and counterpunch. Soon the rebuttals chipped away at Dole's credibility and made him seem to be an increasingly negative campaigner. Dole's capacity to throw negatives eroded as his credibility ebbed and his candidacy died.

As in the Asian art of combat by jujitsu, Dole's strength became his biggest enemy. The more he hammered at Clinton, spending millions to pound home doubts about the president's character and sincerity, the more he came to be seen as negative, surly, nasty, sour, old, and cranky. Clinton's constant accusations that his opponent was running a negative campaign sullied Dole's image, while the GOP ads unintentionally pounded Clinton's message home.

Frequently, however, voters can believe all the negatives that are thrown at a candidate and still vote for him.

In 1996, the GOP hit Clinton as a man of weak character. They said that his move to the center of the ideological spectrum was politically motivated and insincere, and that his administration was mired in scandal. Unflattering comments all, but none was decisive in tipping the election against the incumbent. Voters largely agreed that Clinton's character was open to doubt, that his move to the center came from reading the writing on the wall, and agreed that accusations of unseemly conduct abounded. The massive Republican attack persuaded people of these charges. But the charges were not of sufficient gravity to stop people from voting for Clinton.

Likewise, the GOP spent its entire national convention of 1992 hammering at Hillary Clinton, inflicting substantial damage on her image, but leaving her husband—the candidate—relatively unscathed.

Negatives are losing their cachet in American politics. Unanswered, they still reign. But properly rebutted, they explode in the face of their own candidate. Voters have moved beyond them.

CHAPTER 5

Substance over Scandal

T HE SUBTITLE TO THE LEWINSKY SCANDAL and the subsequent unsuccessful attempts to remove Clinton should be, Suppose they gave a scandal and nobody came? The more the GOP reveled in the details of Clinton's behavior, the more revolted Americans became—less at Clinton for his conduct, and more at the GOP for obsessing on it. In the end, it was the Republicans who suffered the most.

Americans are sick of scandal. Apart from the scandal groupies who mainline each salacious item like modern Madame Lafarges knitting while the guillotine falls, most Americans tune out the massive coverage of presidential scandal.

The newsprint devoted to scandal in the past decade likely accounts for about half of the total space allocated to national politics. Iran-Contra, Bush-Iraq, and Clinton's passport/Whitewater/travel office/FBI file/campaign finance/Paula Jones/Monica Lewinsky scandals have dominated the time and space TV and print news media allocate to public affairs. Yet Presidents Reagan, Bush, and—at the time of this writing—Clinton have not been particularly ill effected by this massive publicity. After impeachment by the House of Representatives, Bill Clinton's popularity rose by five points. What more proof could be required that voters don't really give a damn?

Voters see scandal totally differently from other issues in our politics. They scrutinize the way an elected official votes on any number of issues. They evaluate who is contributing to his campaign. They want to know what special-interest groups are for and against him. But voters pay very little attention to allegations of scandal in sizing up a politician unless those allegations are signed, sealed, delivered, and proven. When the cops cart him off to jail, they draw adverse conclusions. Until then, they won't even look at the evidence in most cases. Voters have seen too many charges about too many good people to be influenced by an allegation. Even when the details of the scandal play out luridly on television night after night, the average voter says to the TV screen, "Wake me when you have proof."

The electorate is very conscious of the separation of powers. The voters are there to decide if a candidate is to their liking. A jury is there to decide if he did anything wrong. People are not willing to banish a man from public life based on media accounts unless formal criminal charges have been filed. Once a politician is indicted, and certainly after he is convicted, voters turn away from him. But not before.

Sex scandals occupy a particularly low place in the electorate's esteem. As the media pries deeper, with less compunction, tact, or decorum than ever before, voters are determined to ignore more and more of what the hounds of the press dig up. Ironically, even as voters are fed a daily diet of sex scandal, they react more benignly than ever before. While American politicians must suffer massive invasions of their privacy, these intrusions have less and less consequence.

The exception is when the conduct involves something other than illicit private sexual conduct. Voters will not forgive child abuse, sexual assault, proven instances of sexual harassment, a failure to pay child support, or spousal violence. They will forgive adultery, out-of-wedlock children, and—in some states—homosexuality.

Again, the transition to a Jeffersonian model of direct, as opposed to representative, democracy has a lot to do with the decreasing importance of scandal. Voters are a lot less concerned about the abstract qualifications a candidate might have than they are about what he will do to help them in their own personal lives. They are much more likely to judge a candidate on how he focuses on their problems than on how they assess his qualifications or attributes.

A careful analysis of the polling during Clinton's first term suggests that the accuser, in most cases, ends up with more egg on his face than his target. Senator Alfonse D'Amato suffered enormous damage to his popularity in New York state after his performance as chairman of the Senate committee investigating Whitewater and the Vince Foster suicide. He never recovered, and the negative ratings he racked up were crucial in his defeat for reelection in 1998.

The job ratings of the Republican Congress during the 1997–1998 session were dismal as it wallowed in scandal investigations. After initially avoiding involvement in the Monica Lewinsky scandal, the Republicans jumped in with both feet as the election of 1998 approached. Their poll numbers had been rising throughout 1998 as they skirted the Lewinsky scandal. Between January 1998 and April 1998, the percentage of voters who had a favorable opinion of Congress rose from 35 percent to 49 percent. But once Special Prosecutor Kenneth Starr laid his findings before the Congress and the GOP began to run ads attacking Clinton for the scandal, the positive ratings for Congress evaporated and the GOP suffered reversals in the 1998 election.

Voters simply do not regard the possible corruption of one's political adversaries as belonging in the electoral process. They feel strongly that the investigation and prosecution of political corruption should stay in the realm of police, district attorneys, judges, and juries, not on the agenda of political candidates.

When parties or candidates base their campaigns on anticorruption issues without judicial proof that they are correct, they are shooting blanks. When each day's press release expresses shock at the scandals of the other party, rather than focusing on issues like tobacco, drugs, crime, day care, and so forth, the party will win no support from the voters.

While the voters have turned off scandal, the political parties haven't gotten the message. The Democrats have never quite gotten over their good fortune in the Watergate scandal. Congressional Republicans are forever trying to reenact the Jim Wright scandals of the 1980s, which forced the Democratic Speaker from office and laid the groundwork—in the GOP's view—for the Republican takeover of the House.

But the Nixon and Wright affairs took place dozens of scandals ago. The cumulative effect of endless investigations has been a dulling of voter interest and sensitivity, and a tendency to delegate scandal-monitoring to the judicial branch where it belongs.

The steady diet of scandal about both political parties makes those voters who read the daily fare of exposé cynical toward Democrats and Republicans. Seeing no monopoly of virtue in either party, they suspect both of corruption. Often, they feel an "honest" politician is just someone whose scandalous conduct has yet to be exposed. Not having someone to vote for and finding only someone to vote against, scandal lacks political relevance.

The media runs with scandal on its nightly news because it marches to the beat of a different drummer. Media outlets don't care about swing voters, they worry about ratings. It doesn't matter to ABC-TV if the viewers it attracts are base Democrats, base Republicans, or Independents. Hard-core partisans love scandals that afflict the other party. Right-wingers luxuriate in Clinton's scandals, while liberals can't get enough of any malfeasance involving Newt Gingrich. Scandal sells newspapers, radio programs, and TV shows. It just doesn't move voters. It attracts those who are already decided politically—base voters of either party—to the TV set, but it does little to influence the real playing ground of our politics: the independent middle.

CHAPTER 6

Strategy over Spin

SPIN IS OVERRATED. It is strategy, not spin, that wins elections. By an obsessive focus on the next day's news coverage, candidates often lose sight of the need to make their issue stick, which is the central dynamic of the race. Getting short-term advantage out of each day's media through spin is like playing checkers, while winning the clash of ideas through strategy is like playing chess.

Members of the media, who follow the moment-to-moment play of politics, worry a lot about spin since they watch its formulation and implementation up close. But voters who want to know more about how a candidate's policies will affect them are more interested in substance and issues than in the daily ebb and flow of who is up and who is down.

A candidate or consultant who waits for the other candidate to make a mistake or relies on outspending his opponent to win is playing a fool's game. The wiser course is to rely on a basic strategy which frames the interplay of competing messages clearly and shows a path to victory.

A good campaign strategy may take months to formulate, but it should take no more than a few words to express. We can explain all recent successful presidential campaign strategies simply.

Truman '48: Tie the Neanderthal Republican Congress around the neck of their largely progressive presidential candidate, Thomas E. Dewey, and rekindle the passions that animated the New Deal.

Eisenhower '52: Capitalize on discontent with corruption, domestic communism, and the stalemate in Korea to show this honest former general to best advantage.

Eisenhower '56: Emphasize the fact that under the first Republican administration in a generation, America is experiencing peace with property.

Kennedy '60: Capitalize on the national sense of drift and the insecurity generated by the Soviet space and missile program to make the case for a sharp departure from Eisenhower policies.

Johnson '64: Make people scared to death of Barry Goldwater.

Nixon '68: Exploit mainstream resentment against the Johnson-Humphrey administration, the Vietnam War, and the Democrats, and say as little as possible about what Nixon's alternative would be.

Nixon '72: Kindle a social populist base by exploiting resentment against leftist hippies and tapping into Southern and Northern racism.

Carter '76: Use Carter's smile and goody-goody image to underscore Ford's connection with Nixon and his pardon.

Reagan '80: Blame America's economic and international weakness on Carter's personal weakness. Contrast his worry about a national "malaise" with Reagan's optimism and buoyancy.

Reagan '84: Drain the ideology from Reagan's image and use economic recovery to make him seem a universal figure. Tie Mondale to Carter.

Bush '88: Fill the vacuum of information about Dukakis with liberal, unpopular positions of which he was proud, and contrast them with a firm—if insincere—pledge of "no new taxes."

Clinton '92: Move to the right of the Democratic Party's traditional positions on welfare and crime and use economic discontent to portray Bush as stagnant and Clinton as filled with optimism and energy.

Clinton '96: Co-opt the center by consensus positions on balancing the budget, education, and welfare, and force Dole to defend extreme GOP views on guns, abortion, tobacco, family leave, and Medicare. Label Clinton's positions as "new" and Dole's as "old" to underscore the age difference.

All it takes is a sentence. But it is a sentence most campaigns never write. Instead, they wait to see what develops, hoping to pounce on tactical errors such as an opponent's failure to debate or a misstep on the campaign trail. Often, especially in the Republican Party, campaigns confuse ammunition with strategy. "We'll keep firing the negatives until we run out," is sometimes the plan.

But strategy must involve a basic approach and theme which takes account of the public mood, the opponent's weakness, and one's own strength. Politicians must think five or six moves ahead, anticipate the other side's response, and program alternate moves in reply. The key is to fix one's attention rigidly on the horizon and hammer at the campaign message and theme. A candidate must use every issue, event, attack, and rebuttal to make the basic point again and again and not let spin or targets of opportunity lure him away from his message. Instead, he must incorporate them into his theme.

When Dole resigned from the Senate in 1996 to run for president as an "ordinary, private citizen," Clinton's campaign struggled to regain its stride. The campaign answered with an ad conceived by media consultant Marius Penczner, which showed moving crates and boxes piled high on the senator's now-empty desk. The announcer said, "He said he would lead. He said he'd cut taxes. Said he'd balance the budget. Reform welfare. But now he's quitting to run a negative campaign against President Clinton. He leaves behind only the gridlock he and Gingrich created. Meanwhile, President Clinton is still on the job, working to balance the budget. . . ." The ad answered Dole's resignation but used the reply to emphasize Clinton's basic theme—always the theme.

Message over money, issues over image, positives over negatives, substance over scandal, strategy over spin—all these trends bode well for our democracy. Candidates can best win elections and can most effectively govern by developing attractive answers to our most pressing problems and dueling with the solutions their adversaries present. Democracy has once again become a dialogue where cogency, persuasiveness, and resonance with the popular will are the keys to winning.

CHAPTER 7

Transcending the Architecture of Parties

AMERICAN POLITICS HAS SETTLED into a pattern in the twentieth century, pitting Democratic compassion against Republican frugality. The donkey's heart battles the elephant's head. Each major political issue inherently skews toward one party or the other. Democrats base their appeal on the four "e" issues: the environment, the elderly, education, and economic growth. The GOP quadrant is crime, taxes, welfare, and fiscal responsibility.

Almost every election features a clash of messages structured along this schematic. A Democrat will plead for more money for schools while a Republican will warn of an impending tax hike. A Democrat will ask for tougher crackdowns on polluters while a Republican will call for more severe measures against street crime. Voters, who dislike both crime and pollution and seek both good schools and low taxes, have to choose which virtue—and which accompanying evil—they want.

This is a crazy way to run a campaign. The way to win is to transcend this architecture, not to invest in it. If a Democrat can keep pace with a Republican on crime, taxes, balancing the budget, and welfare reform, he can use his lead on the four Democratic issues to win.

Voters reject ideology and party politics as models for their decision-making. The greater educational levels and the larger amount of information in play lets voters choose among all the candidates and all their views, without first waiting for a laying-on of hands by a political party or ideology.

The disregard of traditional party agendas was the key to the Clinton victory in 1996. The president pulled even on the GOP issues. Once Clinton had nullified Dole's advantage on the traditional Republican issues, he used his lead on the economy, elderly, environment, and education issues to win the race. Clinton did not win only because he proved as good as the GOP on their base issues. But he avoided losing by doing so. He won on his own issues, but could not have done so as easily if he had sustained damage from Republican attacks over their issues.

The key is to recognize that it is legitimate for Republicans to worry about the elderly, education, and the environment. It is okay for Democrats to work to solve crime and welfare and to hold down taxes. Issues are not the preserve of one party or the other. Candidates, to be effective, need to cross over and show their ability to solve the other side's problems.

Bill Clinton proved this to be so. But the Republicans have yet to realize they can use their basic issues of less taxation and government regulation to win elections only if they offer credible programs for education, the environment, the elderly, and economic growth. But as long as Republicans offer no real alternatives on these Democratic issues, voters will continue to reject them. Voters will not seek low taxes and limited government at the price of jettisoning their concerns over the Democratic issues.

In addressing the other party's issues, a "me too" campaign never works. To be successful, a candidate cannot just mimic his opponent's rhetoric or programs; rather, he has to invent a new range of solutions to the problems historically associated with the other party. In the 1996 campaign, Clinton did not merely parrot Republican proposals, he sought to defuse the pressure for GOP programs by using Democratic means to achieve Republican goals.

Where the Republicans offered toughness and capital punishment to cope with crime, Clinton offered gun control and hiring extra police to do so. When the Republicans proposed tax cuts across the board, Clinton countered with tax cuts targeting college students, parents of young children, and low-income working people. Clinton adopted GOP welfare reforms calling for time limits on welfare and requiring that recipients work, but added Democratic ideas like tax credits and public works for job creation, more day care, and no cuts in nutritional programs.

Republicans have yet to cross the aisle. They remain content to propose ways to meet their usual partisan goals and tend to resist any environmental programs and any federal education reforms. This is not the way to victory. The right must develop its own solutions using Republican means to achieve Democratic ends.

For example, the right can do a lot to take the education issue away from the left by advocating reform of teacher tenure, teacher testing, and merit pay for teachers. The Democrats, dependent on teacher unions for political support and campaign contributions, will find it hard to agree with these common-sense steps to inject managerial flexibility, performance requirements, and financial incentive into education. The Republicans can have these issues all to themselves.

If Republicans were to back tax cuts to reduce pollution and enhance environmental quality, they would work to preempt Democratic domination of environmental issues. Similarly, if the GOP focused on reducing the tax burdens of the elderly, they could go a long way toward repairing the damage they sustained in the Medicare fight of 1995–1996.

The mandate here is mix and match: Use Democratic means like regulation and spending to achieve goals Republican voters value. Use Republican tools like tax cuts and profit incentives to do the good works Democrats seek.

Democrats must not base their campaigns on asking voters not to worry about crime, high taxes, or welfare, and Republicans cannot ignore the elderly, the environment, or education. The concerns of each side have validity. To win, each side must figure out solutions to the problems targeted by the other side.

CHAPTER 8

Values over Economics

FROM FEDERAL RESERVE BOARD Chairman Alan Greenspan on down, the entire economic superstructure of America is asking the same question: Have we tamed the business cycle? Is there a "new paradigm" of ongoing and continuous slow growth and low inflation?

We don't know yet. But while the current economic climate lasts, Americans have fundamentally shifted their focus from economic concerns to social-values issues. A majority of our countrymen understand that an increase in their disposable personal income is not going to solve the major problems in their lives. Crime, pollution and its health impact, education of their children, time with their families, access to health care, safer foods, cleaner drinking water, and better access to parks and recreation are not going to be improved by a 10 percent rise in take-home pay.

In the days of Theodore Roosevelt and Woodrow Wilson, American politics changed fundamentally from a preoccupation with helping business to one of protecting consumers. Under

Franklin Roosevelt, Harry Truman, and Lyndon Johnson, it evolved once again from assuring fair play in the marketplace to actively assuring economic security. Now, a third transformation is under-way—from guaranteeing economic minimums to catalyzing lifestyle improvement.

The new challenges our politics must address are less economic than social, and their remedies relate more to changes in attitudes and mores than to increases in public spending. While improvements to the environment and law enforcement cost money, the main stuff of federal budgets—income redistribution and cash transfer—is no longer on the cutting edge of our political agenda. Our political season is increasingly less defined by the beginning and end of the federal fiscal year. National goals are less matters of dollars than of values, and government action is increasingly to encourage and offer incentive, not to subsidize.

President Clinton's success in maintaining his high job approval rating reflects his ability to articulate these concerns and to recognize the new issues of our political process. Consider the values-oriented proposals that have buoyed his popularity:

- extending family leave
- banning handgun ownership for those arrested for domestic abuse
- expanding child care
- tax credits for college tuition
- testing for educational standards
- increased school construction
- extra police on the streets
- more help for the disabled
- increased funding for disease prevention
- more rapid cleanup of toxic wastes
- increases in clean air standards

- better food safety inspection
- cleaner drinking water
- cleanup of urban brownfield sites
- keeping schools open late as community centers
- incentives for organ donations
- standards for home healthcare workers
- bans on cigarette advertising aimed at teenagers
- tracking gun ownership across state lines
- tracking sex criminals after release from prison
- promoting educational content on children's TV
- rating systems for violence and sex on television
- drug counselors in schools
- doubling of Head Start programs
- a federal DWI standard
- more vigorous child-support collection
- preservation and reform of affirmative action, eliminating quotas
- incentives for employment of welfare recipients
- tax credits for adult education at community colleges
- child immunization
- school bus safety
- curfews for teenagers
- school uniforms

These proposals and dozens more of the same genre are the new stuff of our politics. To political leaders steeped in the focus on incomes and distribution of wealth, the list seems trivial. But to Americans faced with the daily, daunting task of raising a family, the list spells *H-E-L-P*—a day-to-day aid in overcoming the obstacles they face in building a better life.

Political figures in modern America need to dig themselves out of their economic determinism, put away their Marx and their

Charles and Mary Beard, and focus on the social needs of their constituents. This expanded focus of public activity is the new agenda
voters want to take center stage.

Historically, two types of populism have come to dominate
our politics at various points in the past hundred years. Well defined
by Robert Kazan in his seminal work *The Populist Persuasion*, these
have included three waves of economic populism: the populist farmer
movement in the 1890s, the American Federation of Labor growth
in the early years of this century, and the industrial unionization in
the 1930s—and four waves of social populism: Prohibition in the 1920s,
McCarthyism in the 1950s, the New Left in the 1960s, and George
Wallace in the 1970s. Each of these movements were fueled by anger
and focused on an enemy.

But the new values agenda leaves populists without a cause.
The economic populism of the left—which hates Wall Street—and
the social populism of the right—which hates social diversity—have
very little to do with most of these new issues. In fact, the anger
which impels populism, the politics of resentment, is stylistically
inappropriate for our new public priorities. The fundamentally negative proposals of the economic left (anti-corporate privilege, anti-
speculator profiteering) and the equally negative ideas of the social
right (anti-gay rights, anti-choice, anti-immigrant) have nothing to
do with the largely positive proposals of the new agenda.

In the elections of 1992 and 1994, Americans were fueled
first by economic and then by social populism. Angered by the recession of 1991, which lingered in our politics long after the economy
resumed its sluggish growth, they voted first against Bush by backing
Clinton, and then against Clinton by backing Gingrich's Republicans. But after the 1994 elections, the politics of populism faded in
our culture. Now, our politics marches to the beat of a different drummer. Basically, the new American issues are moved by compassion,

not anger, more by love than hate. Our people are more inclined to vote for than to vote against, a sharp reversal from the anger of the 1970s and the self-involvement of the 1980s.

Since voters do not want to topple establishments, just help children and families live better, the era of *the big issue* has left us. It went the way of big government. No overarching ideological redesign of our basic economic, social, or tax systems is going to galvanize today's voters.

By its very nature, the new agenda consists of small bricks of progress, each a good idea, most of them stemming from consensus, and all aimed in a positive direction to improve people's lives in specific but small ways. Yet in the aggregate, these bricks combine to build an impressive edifice of social change to improve the lives of the average American.

CHAPTER 9

Women and Children First

T HE TRADITIONAL HIERARCHIC PYRAMID of our politics has been turned upside down. Where once men came first, women second, and children last in our political focus, the order is now reversed. Political agendas which focus on the needs of children are the most compelling. The social concerns of women for their families rank a close second.

Richard Nixon taught America that crime was a national issue. At times, it seemed as if it was *the* national issue. Bill Clinton has taught us that education is one of the most important national issues. No longer are schools a political backwater for state races. They are the substance of our national political agenda and the focus of our electorate. Ten years ago, education ranked first or second on the list of issues facing a state, but public-opinion pollsters found that it ranked far down as a federal problem. Current polls place education at the very top of our national-issue concerns and priorities.

As the political focus shifts from economic concerns of businessmen to the social concerns of mothers and fathers, a curious dichotomy commands our attention. The interest groups which dominate our legislative process overwhelmingly concern the older economic agenda. Few lobbyists prowl the halls of Congress fighting for child nutrition or foster care reform or higher educational standards. Those who do tend to represent unions seeking their own economic interests, not the social needs of the children they are supposed to serve.

So an American politician faces a situation where his nine-to-five day is likely to be occupied with the push and pull of economic interests in battles that do not really concern his constituents much. The average American doesn't really care about the wars of doctors versus trial lawyers, big banks versus regional banks, AT&T versus MCI, national phone companies versus local Bell spin-offs, cable companies versus phone companies. For the most part, voters don't have a horse in any of these races. But the issues that *do* rivet their focus are not the central issues over which these warring special interests contend. A politician must make time in his day to work on the things his constituents care about. Unless he deliberately turns aside from these commercial dogfights and involves himself in issues on which the lobbyists are silent and uninterested, his political focus will wander far from his voters' concerns.

Even among human-services issues, the lobbying guns are all lined up for the elderly. The American Association of Retired Persons (AARP)—of which I became a direct-mail target when I turned fifty—is one of the most potent lobbies around. But voters care more about the very young than the old. The 1960s focus on elderly poverty has given way to a sense that we are neglecting our children while we subsidize our seniors. With a quarter of America's children growing up in poverty (twice the proportion of the population as a whole), voters want to hear more about the under-five set than about those over eighty.

One of the blind spots of the Republican Party is the increasing concern American voters have for the working poor—those not on welfare but still in or near poverty. One of the major mistakes of their Contract With America was its opposition to the expansion of the earned-income tax credit, initially passed under Republican presidents, which assures the working poor of federal tax credits and subsidies to lift them out of poverty. Public concern has shifted from the bottom 10 percent, who are on welfare, to the next 10 percent, who are working but struggling to make it.

These new foci of our politics turn our old interest-group priorities on their heads. The very groups for whom no lobbyist speaks are those the voters most want our process to hear. From this paradox emerges the true ideological fault line of modern politics: the insider versus the outsider. No longer is the left/right division the most important. Voters see little difference between the right-wing friends of doctors and the left-wing friends of trial lawyers. They are both insiders. The electorate wants politicians who will speak up for four-year-old children, single mothers leaving welfare to find a job, or low-income men anxious to upgrade their skills and improve their jobs. These interests do not donate money. They have no trade associations to advance their goals. They don't even vote in large numbers. But their problems galvanize those who do vote and play a central role in our elections.

CHAPTER 10

Generosity over Self-Interest

F VOTERS APPRECIATE that the major issues in their lives are social rather than economic, they also realize that their own individual self-interest can best be served by helping others.

Pollution can best be prevented by policing industry and by enlightening the public. Education can best be served by upgrading standards in schools and funding them. Welfare and taxes can best be reduced by improving educational and vocational opportunities for the poor and making them find work or go to school. Crime can best be addressed by arresting criminals and by helping young people stay out of crime.

None of these steps involves any program, subsidy, or tax cut that is in the direct economic interest of the vast bulk of the voters. Not one of these ideas will put more money into their pockets, yet they are the key initiatives voters agree are vital to improving their personal quality of life.

So, enlightened self-interest may have achieved what religion never has done in leading the American voter to value charity and generosity to others over padding his own pocket.

But our politicians, as always, are slow to get the message.

When Bob Dole's advisors suggested he propose a 15 percent personal income tax cut across the board, they felt he had a sure winner in the idea. Working from a playbook from the early 1980s, they hoped that voters would realize that Dole's idea meant more money in their paychecks every week.

But they misunderstood the voters. The electorate knew that a tax cut would help each of them personally. But they also knew that a fatter paycheck was not their major priority. Their self-interest led elsewhere. They understood that their lives would be made better by helping others than by helping themselves.

So Clinton's smaller but targeted tax cut carried the day. Voters wanted to cut the taxes of parents with children living at home. They liked tax credits for kids going to college, or adults returning for retraining and additional schooling. The electorate supported tax breaks to make it easier for first-time homebuyers to save for a down payment and for people to save for college.

"Give the money to *them*, not to *me*," the American voter said, shocking the political establishment. Voters have become generous because they realize that only by helping others can they make their communities safe and stable.

In the cold, objective world of practical politics, we must come to realize that warm hearted generosity, with standards and discipline, is the most pragmatic course for a politician to pursue. What virtue doesn't prompt, a candidate's self-interest should elicit.

Environmentalism most effectively captures this sense of helping oneself by helping others. As Americans worry about their diet, drinking water, and air, they've become aware that the pollution that hurts their neighbor also hurts them. As environmentalism turns its focus to global problems like ozone depletion and planetary warming, the self-interest evident in working with others becomes ever more apparent. The dangers of pollution and climate change mock the basic construct of self-interest politics. Is there any CEO who wants to die young as he breathes our common air?

The illogic of self-centered politics is dawning on large numbers of Americans, but not on their political candidates. But as the global problems of environmental destruction loom ever larger, it is inevitable that the twenty-first century will become more preoccupied with common interest than with self-interest.

CHAPTER 11

Communities, Not Governments

IF THE AGENDA of our politics has changed, so has the means of achieving it. It is almost a truism to say that politics concerns itself with the direction of government. But this statement is no longer really true. Most of the important changes our new electorate seeks can best be addressed through collective community action, often using the marketplace and profit incentives to advance their goals. Government's role in this new vehicle for change is to organize, publicize, catalyze, and—sometimes—partially to subsidize. It is not to bureaucratize.

For a long time, political theorists have spoken about the need for more industrial democracy, empowering workers in the management of the businesses that employ them. But voters are now seeking a kind of marketplace democracy in which they can use their economic power, just as they do their electoral franchise, to promote social changes.

In its elemental stages, this new form of political power has already arrived. Recycled toilet paper sells better than the perfumed, pink, soft, double-ply alternative that comes from dead trees. "Biodegradable" (meaning that it rots) was once a product's downfall. Now, it is its most treasured attribute. The changes triggered by worldwide disinvestment in South Africa show the power of a marketplace determined to trigger social change. Swiss bankers are doing whatever they can to avoid a global boycott over their hoarding of ill-gotten gains from Nazi bank accounts.

Increasingly, politicians should look to schemes that harness the positive social intentions of American consumers to the task of upgrading their world. Recently, a consortium of timber producers sought to label their wood so that purchasers of their end product would know that they had observed all the suggestions of environmental and wildlife preservation groups in their lumbering practices.

Former Secretary of Labor Robert Reich has proposed an idea that may well be the blueprint for scores of schemes to use the profit motive to induce social change. He proposes that the apparel industry either adopt voluntarily, or have adopted for them, suggested minimum standards for working conditions and compensation of workers, and prohibit child labor. Then he suggests that any garment manufacturer who complies with the standards and is willing to open his factories to inspection be permitted to buy "No Sweat" labels to sew into his merchandise for consumers to see. The revenues from the sale of the labels would pay for the inspectors and for advertising to urge consumers to buy only No Sweat garments.

Would China permit American inspectors to examine their garment factories? Not on your life. But denied the No Sweat label, they would likely see their American market share plummet and be forced to relent. Beijing would never succumb to government pressure to violate its sovereignty to open its factories, but in the face of pressure from the American marketplace, it would indeed be helpless to prevent it.

This generic formula can work in many different situations. First, formulate standards for an industry to follow voluntarily. Then, publicly reward cooperating companies so that consumers can tell which are their products. Finally, publicize their compliance and then sit back and let the marketplace do its work:

- Which banks have safe cash machines?
- Which HMOs permit patients to appeal denials of treatments?
- Which TV programs and movies have especially good educational or values content?
- Which toys are safest and most educational for children?
- Which foreign imports have been made by workers paid most fairly?
- Which schools have been certified to have the best academic standards?

The key to each of these efforts is that the certification must be by a non-governmental, private, and widely trusted group of people or agencies. The enforcement must be left to the marketplace.

Consumers are clearly willing to pay more for their products if doing so causes positive social change. When Labor Secretary Reich proposed the No Sweat label idea, polling showed that 65 percent of Americans would be willing to pay twenty-five cents more for their garments if they had such a label. By harnessing this desire for idealism and change, a politician can get in sync with the times and can relate to voters in a way that neither the advocates of government intervention nor the supporters of the unfettered marketplace can replicate.

Proposals like these are the ones that will seize the imagination of the electorate. They tap into our collective desire for progress without regulation and for social change without higher taxes.

PART 2

Governing

Our political attitudes have changed how we must govern. The formal powers of the American presidency are increasingly eroded. The Federal Reserve Board, not the president, runs the economy. The American public will not tolerate significant casualties in military action, compromising the president's formal power as commander in chief. With a national mandate to cut taxes and shrink government, new spending is difficult to pass. The national consensus against government regulation further handcuffs the chief executive.

How is a president or an executive leader at any level of government to lead or achieve his agenda? What are the new styles of governance our leaders can use in our new era?

CHAPTER 12

The Need for a Daily Majority

A S WE BECOME more of a Jeffersonian direct democracy, the presidency acquires more of the responsiveness and fragility characteristic of a parliamentary system. No longer does a president get elected and remain powerful for four years. His functional strength ebbs and flows with his popularity as it is measured in weekly tracking polls throughout his term.

Today, a politician does not just need public support to win elections; he needs it to govern. An elected executive—whether president, governor, or mayor—needs a popular majority every day in his term. Politicians and the media ignore titular power and focus only on an elected official's actual ability to command a following. Like canny market traders who disregard face value but look only at the over-the-counter price, they understand that a president without popularity is without power as well. When he dips below 50 percent, he is functionally out of office.

Our constant newspaper polling, instantaneously sensitive to changes in public thinking, has changed the very nature of our democracy. While American presidents do not rise or fall with votes of confidence from Congress like their British counterparts, each week's poll is a vote of confidence the president must win to govern. His only advantage in a nominal hold on the office is that it gives him time to get his popularity back should he lose it.

As scandal took its toll on Nixon and Reagan, Vietnam dogged Johnson, and the economy plagued Bush. All four presidents saw their last years in office robbed of any real power by their drop in popularity. In the language of Watergate, they all twisted slowly in the wind. Bill Clinton took the oath of office on January 21, 1993, but his failure to get even close to a majority of the popular vote cost him much of the power of his presidency in the early years. Buffeted by Whitewater, his executive order on gays in the military, his appointment of Lani Guinier, his failure to get his Attorney General nominees confirmed, the travel office scandal, and even the Los Angeles airport haircut, Clinton found his power eroded from the very beginning. Often, he would say that he felt Republicans "don't recognize me as a real president because I didn't win a majority." When his congressional allies defied the polls and backed the president, passing his 1993 tax increase and backing his health-reform package, it cost them their majority in the 1994 election. It was only when Clinton passed the 50 percent approval mark, after the 1995 government shutdown, that he was really fully empowered as president.

Clinton biographer David Maraniss criticizes the "permanent campaign" that Clinton waged as governor of Arkansas. Many criticized President Clinton's reliance on polling and advertising during the 1995–1996 runup to his reelection. Some will doubtless wonder at the president's ongoing use of polling even as he moves through his second term, unable to seek reelection.

But a politician needs a permanent campaign to keep a permanent majority. One who does not calculate how to keep his support each day over each issue will almost inevitably fail.

In a 1997 panel discussion, *Wall Street Journal* columnist Al Hunt attacked those who bring political manipulation to the White House. "Did Abe Lincoln or Franklin Roosevelt need political handlers?" he asked scornfully at a forum in Washington.

Damn right they did. Their names were David Davis, for Lincoln, and Louie Howe, for Roosevelt. Just as we cleanse the memorials in Washington to keep the marble bright, we sanitize our memories of past political leaders and impute to them a divine streak. But all effective leaders use the tools of persuasion and manipulation to lead and to succeed.

Woodrow Wilson, Franklin Roosevelt, and Harry Truman waged their permanent campaigns from the White House, huddled with advisors Joe Timulty, Louis Howe, Harry Hopkins, and Clark Clifford. Now, a president speaks with political consultants instead. Wilson, Roosevelt, and Truman fought to retain their popularity and sell their programs through barnstorming speeches or radio addresses. Now, a president uses television advertising as well. The icons of the past relied on political instinct. Now, presidents can use scientific polls and focus groups. I fail to see the difference.

In 1978, conservative Democrat Ed King successfully toppled Mike Dukakis as governor of Massachusetts. King lagged badly in the polls throughout the whole campaign, surging only right before primary day and immediately before election day. Dragged down soon after the election by scandal, it was clear the unpopular governor had only two days where he broke 50 percent in popularity— primary day and election day.

They turned out not to be enough. As King's popularity plummeted, the liberal Massachusetts legislature sat on their hands, defeated his programs, and waited him out. Devoid of power, King couldn't get anything passed, which made him an easy target for Dukakis' comeback in the next election.

Keeping a majority does not mean abandoning principle. It means caring enough about how you explain yourself to get the nation behind you. When Franklin D. Roosevelt rallied support for lend-lease by asking if it didn't make sense to lend your neighbor your garden hose if his house was on fire, he overcame America's isolationists. Abraham Lincoln used the biblical metaphor of a house divided against itself to win backing for the eradication of slavery. Woodrow Wilson rallied popular support for America's entry into World War I by calling it a struggle to "make the world safe for democracy." When presidents explain themselves well, they are vindicating principle, not abandoning it.

But when presidents take bold steps and don't explain them properly, they aren't doing their job. Woodrow Wilson's failure to rally popular support for the League of Nations, Jimmy Carter's inability to rescue America from what he called its "malaise," and President Clinton's failure to make a compelling case for his massive healthcare changes are all grisly examples of this failure.

The greater informational levels of the voters, their decreasing inhibitions in expressing disagreement, and their greater preference for Jeffersonian direct involvement all make the need for a "permanent campaign" to sell a president's policies all the more crucial.

After the healthcare debacle, Clinton learned this lesson. It was his permanent campaign—polls, ads, and all—that defined the budget fight against Gingrich as a battle to save Medicare, Medicaid, education, and the environment.

"I won't sit back silently and let them do to me over the budget what they did to me over health reform," President Clinton said at a meeting at the White House in 1995. "We'll be the ones on the air advertising, not just Harry and Louise," alluding to the imaginary couple invented by the insurance companies to attack the president's healthcare plan.

Once upon a time, elections settled things for the term of office. Now, they are mere punctuation marks in an ongoing search for public support and a functioning majority. Each day is election day in modern America.

CHAPTER 13

Whether to Be Aggressive or Conciliatory

MACHIAVELLI ASKED WHETHER it is better to be loved or feared in *The Prince*. The most basic decision a modern politician must make is whether to be aggressive or conciliatory. Should he lash out boldly with new approaches and positions, or focus instead on incremental change? Is it time to run up the flag and charge, or to mediate differences and seek to move the consensus by stages?

Wrongly, a politician's personal temperament or passion usually governs this crucial decision. Rather, it is the mood of the times that should be decisive. The visionary or strident political leader who comes at a time when America yearns for national unity will fall flat. But woe to the leader who seeks sweet reason in a time of national angst and anger. He is usually swept aside by one revolutionary mob or another charging to the left or the right. The conciliator in a time of upheaval will prove inadequate. It matters less if a politician's agenda is great or small, or if his personality is explosive or calm—he must match his style to the mood of his era.

American voters alternate between periods of confrontation and debate and those of moderation and conciliation. During periods of confrontation, we want our political system to describe the alternatives to us and to fashion new answers to coming problems. Unlike Japan, where the political system stresses consensus and candidates rarely articulate sharp differences with one another, Americans want conflict during periods in which we confront new problems and seek new solutions. We egg on the left and the right to fashion agendas and offer their contrasting remedies to what ails us. We welcome one's critiques of the other's proposals as we grope with new questions and national problems.

But there comes a time when our voters have heard enough and are ready to come to conclusions. Impatient with continued debate, they see the consensus they want enacted and feel it is time for their politicians to get on with it. We are not like Italy and France, where debates seem never to come to conclusions, parties remain embittered enemies, and old conflicts keep resurfacing. Here, the left and the right must come together when voters call for consensus and demand that they enact the decisions the people have made. At such times, we Americans will not tolerate divisiveness when it is time for joint action.

Unlike Japan, we use our political system to debate and explore new options when we feel that the conventional wisdom fails to offer adequate solutions. But unlike Italy or France, we do not endlessly polarize our politics into rigid opposing camps. We come to conclusions. Even if our politicians continue to fight, the American people synthesize their views into a national consensus.

In our recent history, the alternating periods of confrontation and conciliation have been clear enough.

While World War II prompted conciliation, postwar uncertainty about the threat of communism, the role of labor, and civil rights triggered a highly partisan polarization in the late 1940s and early 1950s.

The Eisenhower years brought back a calm consensus. Then, concern about racial discrimination, domestic poverty, the war in Vietnam, Watergate, and the energy crisis caused conciliation to fade, ushering in a period of confrontation and change that continued through the early 1980s.

By the middle of the decade, a calm returned under Reagan's seemingly benign stewardship. Shattered by the recession of 1991–1992, debate raged anew as America zigged to the left with Clinton and zagged back to the right with Gingrich. By 1996, the debate was spent and a national mood of bipartisan conciliation and compromise returned.

With each of these oscillations, some politicians got the message and others didn't. For example, Truman, Nixon, and John L. Lewis grasped the combative tenor of the 1945–1953 period and ratcheted up their rhetoric to meet the challenge. But Thomas E. Dewey did not, and came across as too bland and banal.

In the period of consensus that followed, Eisenhower's tone fit well, but the more strident voices like McCarthy's and Nixon's did not. Nixon waited until history came round again to his aggressive style and, with politicians like George Wallace, succeeded well in the turbulent 1960s and 1970s. Those who sought consensus failed. Lyndon Johnson's appeal for wartime unity, Ford's feeble attempt to "Whip Inflation Now (WIN)," and Carter's summons to the "moral equivalent of war" for energy independence didn't work.

If Nixon waited for the times to change to suit his style, Ronald Reagan changed his style to suit the times. In 1980, he reflected national anger and angst by pushing an aggressive agenda of less government and lower taxes. In 1984, he changed his style, morphing into a tone of contentment and prosperity more fitting to the country's mood. Voices of dissent like Gary Hart and Walter Mondale got little attention. Not only were their views too liberal, their style was too aggressive and activist to suit the pacific mid-1980s.

When recession broke the calm, Bill Clinton profited by the new intensity of the debate, while President George Bush vainly sought to ride the feelings of national harmony after they had vanished. In the 1992 campaign, the incumbent's assurance that the recession had passed, and his appeals for national unity, sounded hollow in a country that demanded activist answers to nagging and deepening problems.

After he took office, Clinton rode the polarization of the national debate with an aggressively liberal program of tax increases and healthcare reform. It was Newt Gingrich's genius to counter the activism of the left with that of the right. Realizing that the times were neither liberal nor conservative, but simply activist, he achieved control of Congress in 1994 with aggressive advocacy of spending and tax cuts, opposition to gun control, and a pro-life agenda on abortion.

As the Gingrich budget cuts wore thin on America, Clinton's liberal advisors urged him daily to lash out at Republican cuts in school lunches and Medicare. Speechwriting at the White House became a search through the thesaurus for new invective. Clinton scorched Republican policies. But his ratings remained dismal and the hot words seemed only to dig him deeper into his hole.

Like Reagan before him, Clinton came to realize that the national mood had again shifted. Exhausted by the liberal extremism of healthcare reform and the right-wing agenda of harsh budget cuts, the nation wanted its politicians to get together and compromise their differences. His overtures to Gingrich in the aftermath of the GOP 1994 victory were well received in the polls, but his aggressive condemnation of the Republican cuts did little to improve his popularity.

America was not in the mood for another fight. Having steered left with Clinton and right with Gingrich, it now wanted compromise. Only when the president cast aside what he called "the liberal stuff my staff keeps putting in front of me every day," and outlined a way to balance the budget and cut taxes without slashing vital programs, did America begin to listen.

As Clinton lowered his voice, he raised his ratings. When he crossed party lines to advocate a balanced budget and fashioned a compromise on welfare reform, he moved into the ascendancy. President Clinton's recognition that the nation wanted compromise and "common ground" in 1995 and 1996, while the Republican right and the Democratic left spoiled for one more decisive round of conflict, impelled his turnaround in fortune and his reelection.

When Trent Lott inherited the Senate Republican leadership in mid-1996, he realized that the national mood had shifted back to a desire for consensus and unity. Understanding that the GOP had moved too far toward confrontation, he understood that he could not keep the Senate in GOP hands without setting aside partisanship and turning to compromise. When he took power, he noted that most incumbent Republican senators faced uphill battles for reelection. "Forget about it if we don't start passing some laws around here," Lott said. When he worked with Clinton to pass the minimum-wage increase, the Kennedy-Kassenbaum law, and welfare reform, he saw his GOP congressional incumbents rise in the polls. Consensus worked.

A political leader should take the temperature and monitor the pulse of the times in which he lives. With humility, he must tailor his style of advocacy to his findings. He need not mute his desire for change or modify his ideas, but he must make sure his style matches the public's mood.

A political leader can realize far-reaching goals even when the times call for moderation. The far-reaching reform Clinton failed to achieve in his 1994 healthcare legislation happened incrementally through the private sector and through gradual expansion of healthcare coverage to children.

A leader in a conciliatory era need not limit his goals, he must just lower his voice and take smaller steps. The leader who indulges his own personality, whether angry or conciliatory, at the expense of matching the public's mood, is guilty of hubris.

Eventually, of course, bipartisan consensus runs its course. Once the consensus has been enacted, new problems inevitably arise, leading to new issues and new polarities. Then, Americans will welcome the debate and urge each party to offer its solutions. The style of politics changes, and those who seek consensus and unity will be left behind until the cycle comes back around to them or until they change their styles to fit the public's mood.

In our own time, after bipartisan agreements to balance the budget, cut taxes, reform welfare, and preserve Social Security are consummated, the politics of moderation and consensus will likely exhaust its mandate. New issues will come to the fore and generate new controversies. Among them will be HMO regulation, IRS supervision, reform of public education and teacher tenure, curbing drug and alcohol use by teenagers, paying for college, expanding leisure time, curbing TV sex and violence, regulating genetic engineering, and a host of others. Democracy will be renewing its relevance.

CHAPTER 14

How to Lead

IN HIS MEMOIR of the Ford administration, Henry Kissinger articulated the key mandate for any elected official: "A statesman's job is to bridge the gap between his vision and his nation's experience. If his vision gets too far out ahead of his country's experience, he will lose his mandate. But if he hews too close to the conventional, he risks losing control over events."

Leadership is a dynamic tension between where a politician thinks his country must go and where his voters want it to go.

Bold initiatives that leave the voters behind are not acts of leadership but of self-indulgent arrogance. Clinton's healthcare reform plan of 1993, Roosevelt's court-packing proposal of 1937, and Wilson's League of Nations campaign in 1919 all entombed good ideas because in each case, the president did not consider his constituents' opinions, only his own.

The answer is not to abjure change but to seek it with political wisdom. Timid, tepid, meek governance leaves the initiative to others—usually enemies—and reduces a political leader to a gambler, dependent on good times and dumb luck to take him where he wants to go. Bush's economic non-program of 1991 and Clinton's early non-policy in Bosnia illustrate how presidents who lack an agenda also fail.

The art of leadership is to maintain sufficient forward momentum to control events and steer public policy without losing public support. In the past, politicians had to rely on intuition to succeed in this balancing act. Lincoln needed to figure out when he could emancipate the slaves without losing the border states. Roosevelt had to calibrate finely how he could overcome isolationism and calculate how far he could go to help the Allies without risking a massive backlash. Kennedy had to monitor the extent of public outrage over racial discrimination before he could risk losing the South by advocating civil-rights legislation.

Just as the computer has replaced the abacus, the fax machine has replaced the messenger and the telephone has made the telegraph obsolete, so public-opinion polling is substituting quantification for guesswork in enabling leadership.

Polling does not replace leadership. A politician who "governs by polls" would fail Kissinger's test. He would "lose control over events." But one who ignored polls would "lose his mandate." With our Jeffersonian democracy, voters want to play a larger and larger role in determining the outcomes of our political debate. They expect to be heard, and polling is the way we translate their opinions into a language that politicians can understand.

Political opportunists won't do anything that is unpopular. Idealists will do unpopular things, but they almost insist on martyrdom. Pragmatists know they often have to embrace positions that the public doesn't like, but they work hard at articulating their views so as to survive to fight again another day.

The key is to integrate leading and polling in a dialogue to settle on the right proposal in the best form at the proper time. A leader begins by staking out his ultimate objective, such as balancing the budget, giving all Americans health insurance, upgrading public education, building more roads, or cleaning the environment. There is no substitute for a clear vision and a decisive direction. Carter's and Bush's domestic policies, for example, lacked this sort of definition and never overcame the defect. Reagan and—after initial failure, Clinton—had clear goals and navigated toward them with great success.

A leader must inventory the alternate ways of reaching his objective. With a totally open mind, he needs to reach out for advice on the programs and measures that will get him where he wants to go.

Once he's done his homework, he needs to summon his pollster and walk him through the options, possibilities, and alternatives. For each, he must figure which arguments bolster and which damage his proposal. It has been Clinton's great strength that his endlessly fertile mind is constantly inventing new alternative programs to reach his goals and quickly grasps the possible arguments for and against each idea. He briefs his pollsters for hours on the options he wants them to probe. A good pollster then tests each specific alternative, examining the arguments for and against to measure public support.

An idealistic leader will not hesitate to do something that is unpopular. But a smart idealist will carefully measure public opinion before he does so and will develop a strategy to persuade the electorate. Our sophisticated American electorate will come around if a leader takes the time to understand the concerns of his voters and addresses them articulately and well. In this way, polling makes strong leadership possible.

Frequently, President Clinton's views differed sharply from those of the American people. For a president said to "govern" by polls, it is ironic how many unpopular positions he has taken. It only seems that he is dominated by surveys because he uses them to figure out, as he did when he sent troops to Bosnia, how to make the unpopular palatable.

When Clinton decided to send twenty-five thousand ground troops to Bosnia to enforce the peace, he knew that his formal power to order them into action meant little. Without a majority behind him, he knew Congress could easily curtail funding or use the War Powers Resolution to force withdrawal. Without the backing of a congressional and popular majority, the commander in chief was the "helpless, pitiful giant" of Nixon's rhetoric.

So, President Clinton won popular support for the Bosnia deployment using the polling and media of the permanent campaign. Surveys indicated that Americans opposed sending troops by 35 percent to 55 percent. But the polls also showed that voters didn't know what the troops were going to do once they got there. The voters envisioned search-and-destroy missions through the mountains of Bosnia, summoning the worst memories of the Vietnam War. But polling showed that when voters learned the troops would only police borders, not search the mountains for war criminals, support swelled to a majority. The president used a national TV address to explain the Bosnia mission and to differentiate warmaking from peacekeeping. With public support assured, Congress became compliant. Clinton got to send his troops and was reelected anyway.

At times, a leader can use a popular position to counter an unpopular one. When Clinton decided to oppose a balanced budget amendment to the Constitution despite heavy majorities favoring it, he stepped up his efforts to actually balance the budget. Similarly, Clinton sought to escape blame for his opposition to a very popular school prayer amendment by publicizing to schools the steps they could take right now to enhance spirituality in education without violating the First Amendment and without changing the Constitution. Once school boards realized they could have moments of silence, religious clubs after hours, courses on morality and ethics, and other forms of values education without amending the Constitution, few voters saw the need for a constitutional amendment.

When a policy is unpopular, a leader often has to change it to save it. In 1985, President Reagan had to recant his initial tax-reform proposal to eliminate deductions for state and local taxes in order to win approval of his overall package. In the summer of 1995, Clinton bolstered the effort to preserve racial and gender affirmative action programs by changing them. Realizing that conservative sentiment to repeal affirmative action was on the rise, he bowed to the need for reform. "Mending" the program rather than "ending" it, he prohibited racial or gender quotas, insisted that no dismissals ever be required by affirmative action, and required that all people hired by an employer to comply with affirmative action be fully qualified.

Most frequently, the key to taking unpopular actions is to be precise in justifying them with popular specific arguments. Clinton suffered no damage from twice vetoing welfare-reform legislation because he quite clearly enumerated the defects of the bill before him. By focusing public attention on the lack of day care, cuts in school lunches, and slashes in Medicaid, he rallied political support for a veto of a bill whose essential welfare-to-work provisions were highly popular. When the legislation was amended to eliminate the offending parts, he signed it.

A leader must take care to stand on solid ground when he does something the voters don't like. Reagan failed to do so when he proposed limiting cost-of-living adjustments for Social Security payments, saying only that we had to cut spending in order to cut taxes. But when Clinton urged a similar reduction, he succeeded by convincing the nation that the cost-of-living index exaggerated inflation and needed to be updated to suit modern economic realities. He succeeded in portraying the cut as a technical correction.

As a senator from the tobacco-producing state of Tennessee, Al Gore supported requiring warning labels on cigarette packs even though the industry fiercely opposed the idea. Gore explained that he based his position on the need to discourage kids from smoking and, with that argument, won the forgiveness of his tobacco farmer constituents. "I'd go out to tobacco country and speak in front of all these farmers in overalls and I'd ask them if they wanted their kids to smoke. They'd shake their heads no and I'd say, 'That's why we need these warning labels.' On that basis, it was okay with them."

Too often, leaders don't think carefully before they take unpopular positions. Intellectually lazy, it's easier to revel in martyrdom (on the one hand) or to resort to demagoguery (on the other hand) than to think out in advance how to take an unpopular position . . . and survive. A politician can do what he thinks is right, he just has to be sophisticated in how he goes about it.

Those who seek a president who "will disregard the polls and just lead," ask for the political equivalent of *The Charge of the Light Brigade* (" . . . theirs not to reason why, theirs but to do or die"). It does no service to a cause to fail grandly.

When Clinton called for massive healthcare reform, he failed to use polling and leadership properly. The president understood that managed care had to come to America and that we would have to acquiesce in the abridgment of our historic prerogative of choosing our own doctors and courses of treatment. But Clinton never realized how unpopular this course would be. He should have left it alone. Ironically, a few years after his proposal had died, the private sector forced managed care on America, depriving them by employer fiat of the liberties they had valued so highly in rejecting Clinton's plan. Had the president focused his case only on the need to cover all uninsured Americans, without monkeying with the entire system, he'd doubtless have passed his program.

This dialogue between the ideal and the possible must extend to the details of each program or initiative. For example, when President Clinton decided to move toward requiring competency tests for students to upgrade national education standards, he found broad public support. Over 80 percent of the voters agreed that students should be tested and promoted only if they passed the test. But there was a problem. Only 60 percent felt that the federal government should require that states adopt such a system. The fact that Washington required the test robbed the idea of the 20 percent who favored the idea of mandatory testing but wanted the states, not the feds, to impose it.

The president continued the dialogue between policy and polling by suggesting that most states and localities would probably use federally prepared tests if they were offered on a voluntary basis. He felt that pressure from parents and voters on each local school board or on each governor would be so intense that most jurisdictions would adopt the test if only the government designed one. In effect, he echoed the sentiment of the movie *Field of Dreams*, that "if you build it, they will come."

Polls found that voter support for testing for educational standards jumped back to 80 percent when the proposal called for optional, not mandatory testing. The dialogue between policy and polling had found a way to achieve Clinton's goal in a way that worked politically.

Sometimes voters distrust polling because they don't understand it. They think polling is pandering and that disregarding polls is bravery. But this Pickett's Charge school of politics forces a choice between self-destruction and timidity. Neither option is very good government.

CHAPTER 15

Defeating Bureaucratic Inertia

T HE PERMANENT BUREAUCRACY of the executive branch of a democratic government is dedicated to a single mission: To change nothing. Left or right matters little. They are neither liberal nor conservative. They are in favor of things as they are. In pursuit of that mission they are canny, shrewd, ruthless, and conspiratorial. They infiltrate the ranks of those who want change with the goal of destroying them. They use delay and details to overwhelm new ideas and to force a continuation of the status quo.

But the modern electorate demands change and it will not accept failure. A political figure must learn how to overcome bureaucratic inertia and get the policies and results he wants through the bureaucracy.

Bureaucratic opposition to change is particularly deadly since it usually takes place before an idea has made it out into the public arena. It is in this daunting environment of a permanent implacable bureaucratic hostility to change that the public official must formulate his agenda in the first place. It is amid these wolves with bared fangs that he must cultivate initiatives and nurture creative thinking to fruition. Worse, it is from these very agents of obstruction that he has to get the information, data, technical support, legal opinions, budgetary flexibility, and capacity to move personnel, without which no initiative can survive. It is to them that he must turn for logistical support in his efforts to change the system. It's like hiring the wolf to babysit the lamb.

The bureaucracy's weapons to stifle change are truly intimidating. The first line of defense is usually delay and obfuscation. Memos get lost. Demands for information get sidetracked.

Bureaucrats also tend to use crises to block initiatives for change. When a crisis comes at you, all the affirmative changes you seek must wait while a confrontation of someone else's choosing on someone else's ground plays out. Do you want to raise educational standards in your schools? First you must face down a looming cut in funding. When you ran for office, did you promise welfare reform? You have to wait while we cope with the latest round of federal budget cuts and the resulting rise in the population of the homeless on our streets.

A crisis is almost always a threat to make life worse than the status quo. By forcing the change-oriented executive to defeat deterioration, he needs to sidetrack his commitment to improvement. Indeed, if the threat of things getting worse can remain long enough, an incumbent will get to kind of like the old status quo even if he ran promising to reform it.

A government lawyer is the bureaucrat's bureaucrat. His job is to figure out why change is illegal. Statutes, regulations, and court decisions are his weapons in protecting turf and defeating change.

What the lawyer can't defeat, the technical expert on the staff will try to debunk. Once the technicians have had their crack at stopping change, budget officials and civil service personnel experts take theirs. The entire process is one vast conspiracy to say no.

It would be a mistake to impute any particular ideological bias to a bureaucracy. It is neither liberal nor conservative, it is just against change. Bureaucrats are suspicious of newness simply because they are employed, paid, and not laid off under the oldness. They know how the current system works and fear any new one.

But much of the bureaucracy's animosity to innovation springs from established ways of thinking and time-honored approaches. Each element of the status quo was once a change and likely has its share of champions still on the payroll. If reality has proven their innovation wrong or just dated, few civil servants can escape a sense of personal investment in frustrating changes to the status quo they helped design in their youth.

Above all, civil servants or longtime bureaucrats have no incentive to change. As the providers of service to the public, they can't see the defects in their systems. They won't acknowledge their shortcomings and are sufficiently isolated from the public not to have to acknowledge its frustrations.

The permanent employees of the bureaucracy generally hold their elected and appointed overseers in a certain kind of contempt. Like the children of a frequent divorcée, they regard the current recipient of the electorate's favor as a short-lived flame which will be long extinguished by the time they get around to the days of their own retirement and gold watches. Indeed, many bureaucrats feel their mission is to remain impervious to innovation and to preserve the accumulated body of wisdom their bureaucracy represents against the fashion-conscious intervention of ambitious politicians.

This Edmund Burke-like commitment to stasis impels a bureaucracy to close ranks against the outsider who is nominally their boss. This aversion to catering to the "whims" of each new political leader is especially deep in the military, police, and other uniformed services. With them, resistance to change acquires an almost religious dimension. It takes only one argument to defeat a new idea. A policy proposal must run a gauntlet of criticism, skepticism, and even nihilism to make it out the door. Like a salmon swimming upstream to mate, the odds are decidedly against success.

The following is a very, very partial list of how the mother of all bureaucracies—the federal executive branch—sought to counter initiatives the president wanted during 1995–1996.

Presidential Proposal: That only citizens and legal aliens get driver's licenses, so those who are here illegally can be identified through routine traffic stops.
Counter: The Immigration Service can't handle the extra cases. As the referrals pile up, they will prove a political embarrassment.

Presidential Proposal: That college students get a tax credit to help with tuition costs.
Counter: States will just raise tuition. Tax credits are a poor way to target the needy. Minorities will rebel if we tie the proposal to standards. Whites will rebel if we don't.

Presidential Proposal: To announce the president's support for a stricter blood-alcohol standard.
Counter: Democratic governors will be mad that we didn't consult them.

Presidential Proposal: Federal aid for school construction or renovation.
Counter: Money shouldn't go for brick and mortar. States will just spend less on their own and use federal money instead.

Presidential Proposal: Prohibit people convicted of domestic violence from buying handguns.
Counter: We'll lose police union support because some cops may not be able to get guns.

Presidential Proposal: That homeowners be allowed to sell homes free from capital-gains taxes.

Counter: After signing the welfare-reform bill, we shouldn't give a "goody" to the middle class.

And the list goes on.

Out of pure frustration, an action-conscious political leader must banish all his own doubts. If any doubt creeps into his advocacy of any of his ideas, the forces of the status quo will overwhelm the idea and strangle it in the cradle. It was only by a determined effort to beat back the forces of the status quo that the president was able to salvage his agenda of action from the grip of bureaucracy.

A public official must see the permanent bureaucracy that surrounds him as the enemy of change it is. He must realize that his own appointees are easily captured by the permanent bureaucracy and turned against change. The men and women he puts in public office to facilitate change become subject to "Stockholm syndrome" (that phenomenon observed by psychologists where hostages tend to identify with and defend their captors).

The real solution to bureaucratic obstinacy is to privatize decision-making. Only outsiders can truly facilitate change. An elected official must have his own lawyers, engineers, civil-service experts, and budget people who can provide an alternate way to empower change. If he reaches outside the public sector, can he acquire the logistical support he needs to overcome inertia?

Again, don't let your outside experts get too close to the inside. Aversion to change is contagious. The bureaucratic style of thinking, the endlessly inventive capacity to think up obstacles, can easily overwhelm an expert from the private sector.

An elected official must hang on to the notion that unless he produces change and fulfills his campaign promises, he will likely be out of a job. The energy it takes to keep change on course and bring it through bureaucratic, legal, procedural, political, and financial shellfire is almost superhuman. Yet it is the central challenge of any elected official.

How to Watch Your Back:
Controlling Your Own Party

IN POLITICS, THE MOST LETHAL WOUNDS are inflicted from the rear. The opposing party rarely causes as much angst as does one's own. Any candidate or elected official who seeks to reach beyond his party's base and appeal to the swing voter, upon whom his electoral fortunes depend, invites assault from his own ranks in the rear. In World War II, the Red Army "encouraged" soldiers to charge the enemy and "discouraged" retreat by instructing their rear echelons to shoot anyone of their frontline comrades who turned around to run to the rear. In much the same way, political parties maintain a disciplined adherence to their rigid doctrines by infighting and pressure. When all else fails, they adopt the Red Army approach and shoot those who retreat by challenging them for their own party nomination in primary contests.

In the past, there were very few independent voters. In an era where Gilbert and Sullivan's songs rang true, "Every boy and every girl that is born into this world alive, is either a little liberal or else a little conservative." But the day has passed when elections were duels between rival parties to see who could pull more of their voters to the polls. Elections are decided instead by the 40 percent of the electorate who call themselves "independent," professing no allegiance to either political party.

The needs, desires, dreams, and fears of the independent voter have little in common with those of the party dogmatists who line up on either pole of our politics. The key to reaching these independents is not to follow the party line, but to transcend it. Doing so without feeling cold steel in your back or between your ribs isn't always easy.

The key to controlling your own political party, so that it does not eat you alive, is to realize that while Democratic and Republican leaders differ sharply, their voters do not. The politicians of the two parties are at loggerheads, and their respective special-interest groups are mortal foes of one another, but ordinary Democratic voters and ordinary Republican voters do not differ much.

Except where race is a factor, the difference between Democrats and Republicans on any given issue will rarely exceed twenty-five points. For example, while about 85 percent of Republicans back capital punishment, so do about 70 percent of Democrats. Seventy-five percent of Democrats want to see the minimum wage increased, but so do 55 percent of the Republicans. Even on highly divisive issues like gun control, abortion, gay rights, and affirmative action, the difference between Democrats and Republicans in national surveys is relatively minor.

Even in primary contests, where only the most motivated of a party's voters turn out, there is more consensus among both parties' voters than among their politicians. The plain fact is that Democratic primary voters are far less liberal than Democratic politicians and Republican primary voters are far less conservative than Republican politicians.

However, the sharpest partisan disagreements do not come between politicians of each party, but between the special-interest groups that affiliate with them. If Democratic and Republican voters have more in common than do their respective party politicians, so are these elected officials more in agreement with one another than are the special-interest groups of each political party. Democratic interest groups (feminists, environmentalists, labor unions, trial lawyers, and civil-rights groups) constantly feud with their Republican counterparts (the religious right, the NRA, small-business groups, and right-wing organizations).

To win and to govern successfully, a candidate of either party must take care not to be captured, branded, and held hostage by the extremists and ideologues in his own party. He must transcend party and appeal to the middle. How does he win his party's nomination without catering to the extremes? By realizing that he can go over the heads of the special interests and the politicians and win primaries in his own party by appealing to the more moderate rank-and-file voters. As Bill Clinton proved, leftists don't always win Democratic primaries. And Bob Dole proved rightists don't always win Republican primaries.

The key is to realize the threat one's own party poses to one's career. Their embrace and support may remind one more of a jailer than of a lover.

Bill Clinton began his presidency in 1993, determined to avoid the ineffectuality that had eviscerated Jimmy Carter; he had seen Carter's presidency destroyed by the Democratic barons who controlled Congress. Clinton was determined to cooperate and coordinate with his party's leadership in the House and Senate.

Democratic congressional leaders sent Clinton a simple message: "Abandon your independent ways and we will follow you. Clear everything with our caucus and we will protect you." Clinton had been like a scrambling quarterback during his years as governor and as a presidential candidate. He was used to throwing touchdown passes from anywhere on the field, left or right. He had headed the Democratic Leadership Council (DLC), a group determined to counter the orthodox ways of those who were now asking for Clinton's loyalty. Frightened of ignoring his party and suffering as Carter had for his independence, he set aside his old ways and hunkered down in the quarterback pocket, protected by his party's offensive linemen.

Throughout 1993 and 1994, Republicans got the message that Clinton didn't seem to need or even want their votes. He governed through his party's caucus alone, ignoring GOP senators and congressmen, supposing that their opposition was endemic and inevitable. In fact, it was neither. Republicans rejected Clinton with partisan fury when they saw that he was rejecting them. Faced with de facto exclusion from governing, the Republicans embraced the only course open to them: savage partisanship.

Thus, Clinton was faced with the need to round up every last Democrat, every last liberal, every last stalwart, to pass his programs. The left escalated its demands. When Clinton wanted an essentially conservative anti-crime bill featuring the death penalty and one-hundred thousand extra police for America's streets, Republicans refused to vote for it even though it echoed their own program. Instead, Clinton was forced to seek a virtually unanimous vote of his own party to pass the legislation. To attract the votes of recalcitrant urban congressmen, he had to tack onto the bill all kinds of liberal appropriations for midnight basketball courts and teen recreation centers. Similarly, when Clinton tried to close the deficit through spending cuts, he had to push an economic stimulus package laden with pork to win over blue-collar Democratic votes in the House and Senate. Even though the public liked the central thrust of these Clinton bills, they were turned off by the pork he had to include to get the extra Democratic support.

Soon, Clinton ceased to be the candidate of the Democratic Party and instead became their captive, their hostage. Deprived of support on the right, he was taken over by the left. When the moderate voters throughout the nation saw the "new" Democrat they had elected morphing into a knee-jerk liberal, they deserted him in droves. A vicious cycle ensued where, as more of the moderates left Clinton, he was forced to become more liberal to attract support.

It was only when the Republicans captured Congress that Clinton was freed from his captivity. No longer did his success depend on appeasing Democrats, but on placating Republicans and stealing moderates. So he appealed to the center, amassing sufficient support to abandon the left.

As he began to take this moderate tack, he was shelled from behind by his party faithful. His first balanced budget proposal was voted down in the United States Senate by the embarrassing margin of 0–99. Not a single Democratic senator embraced his spending cuts, tax cuts, or balanced budget. But in time, the popularity of his centrist position grew and made itself felt among the moderate rank and file of the Democratic Party. Soon, Democratic senators were flocking to the president's budget for political cover and jostling with one another for inclusion in photos with the chief executive. Clinton had gone from their captive to their master by moving to the center.

It is from the center that leaders must lead. Each party has its own center, more moderate than its leaders or its campaign donors. By reaching to that center, an elected leader can escape the prison of his own party stalwarts and speak to the bulk of America.

CHAPTER 17

How to Court the Other Party

A N ELECTED OFFICIAL must strengthen his ties with the opposition party to avoid capture by his own. The ability to cross the aisle for votes makes the extremists in one's own party impotent. Since you no longer need their votes to get your program passed, you can ignore their extreme demands and replace those who defect with votes from the other party. A leader who appeals to only one party governs on one leg—an inherently unstable arrangement. You need two legs in order to walk or to govern.

So how does a leader reach across the lines to cultivate the legislators of the opposing party?

The old way was through pork and patronage. While these techniques still work, they have lost much of their utility. Senators and congressmen have been in office for so long that they have come to expect privilege. The opposition is more likely to be outraged if you deny them their regular share of pork than they are to be flattered upon receiving it.

Appealing over the heads of the other party to the voters at home is difficult. Each congressman and senator knows his district or state much better than any president does. To try to take away their base at home is, as Winston Churchill once said of a land war in Asia against Japan, "like going into the water to fight the shark."

The first step is to separate out the two kinds of congressmen and senators: ideologues and men of affairs. The ideological stalwarts march to the beat of their own drummers and value consistency above compromise, purity above pragmatism. They only get in the way.

There is simply no point in trying to court an opposing ideologue. In 1995, ideologues ran the Republican congressional majority. Led by a strong group of right-wing freshmen, the House leadership was hostage to an almost religious demand for fidelity to conservative principles. Because they were not going to compromise, the only way to handle them was to let them walk off a cliff, as they did when they twice shut the government down rather than compromise with Clinton on the federal budget. Only after these ingenues came into contact with the consequences of their own obstinacy and went through the education of running for reelection could one deal with them.

Fortunately, most of the time, a majority of the House of Representatives and the vast majority of the Senate are men of affairs. While ideology is always an element in how they behave, most are more interested in achieving something, getting reelected, and moving ahead. They are professional players. In handling them, one must almost become their political consultant. A leader needs to put himself in the other politician's place and see the world from his vantage point. From this perspective, he should offer political advice calculated to help his partisan adversary see how crossing the partisan aisle can work to his own advantage.

When a Democrat tells a Republican that voting a certain way will get the elderly advocacy groups or the environmental activists off his back, he makes a most potent argument. Republican programs become very attractive to Democrats if they help mollify the animosity of the Christian Coalition or the small-business community.

Fundamentally, Washington is partisan, but America's voters are not. This dichotomy is the single most important difference between the nation and its capital city. In Washington, one is either a Democrat or a Republican. But most voters have grown to dislike both parties more or less equally. These independent voters are the constituency to which a political leader can appeal to bring opposition party legislators into his fold on specific issues and votes.

The problem is that most politicians do not know how to court independents. The vast majority of a candidate's time is spent fighting members of his own party for the nomination. In fighting is far more familiar to the average American politician than is partisan confrontation. For month after month, year after year, he must duel with his colleagues and partisan compatriots for position, privilege, and power. By the time the nomination is his and the general election against the other party is upon him, he usually faces only an eight- or ten-week window where his partisan opposite is his opponent.

Reared in their own party, most politicians don't know enough about independents or the voters of the other party. Most politicians are like Daddy Warbucks. When the Republican tycoon in the musical *Annie* invited FDR to dinner, he asked his secretary to "call Al Smith and find out what Democrats eat." Republicans don't know how to court labor or the other interest groups of the left. Democrats are at sea when it comes to appealing to the right-wing voter or even the right-leaning moderate.

A leader must act as a political consultant or advisor to the legislators on the other side of the partisan divide. He needs to educate them on the likely gains they will score if they cross party lines on a particular vote. A leader needs to explain to a congressman of the opposite party why his views make sense in the electoral arithmetic of his district. Democratic and Republican political professionals both speak this common language better than any other tongue—the language of votes.

But beyond political opportunism and self-interest lies an even more potent appeal: power-sharing. Being a senator or congressman is most often boring. Perpetually forced to vote on other people's initiatives, few of the issues on which they must trudge to the floors of their respective chambers eight, nine, ten, twelve times a day excite much interest in the average legislator. Even the act of voting itself is often illusory. At least nine of every ten votes a member of Congress casts are predetermined by the leadership. Compared to the daily thrill of executive power, the passivity of the average legislative job is maddeningly dull.

Unlike in England, where the top third of the legislators from each party participate either in the actual government or in the shadow cabinet of the opposition, the American legislator normally has no access to executive power. Mired in a legislative rut, his mind wanders constructively to ambition and destructively to corrupting behavior.

So, when the executive opens his doors and lets a member of the other party into the councils of decision-making, a ray of sunlight bursts in on an otherwise bleak existence. Few can resist the temptation or the appeal of relevance and power.

Getting the opposition to help you pass your program can be as easy as opening up and letting them help you formulate it. By admitting the other side into your deliberative process, you win their gratitude and, if you listen carefully to their views, you can amend your course so as to co-opt their support.

An elected leader who wants to score partisan points in anticipation of the next election will obviously find it hard to win the backing of members of the other party. But a leader who is trying to pass legislation can usually count on a fairly broad range of support from the opposite party if he goes about it properly. Not only does this help pass legislation, as we have seen, it confers on the leader an ability to ignore the dictates of the ideologues in his own party.

CHAPTER 18

Special-Interest Groups Are Paper Tigers

T HERE IS NO REASON to fear special-interest groups. They can't deliver the voters they say they can. Sometimes, their support so alienates independent voters that their backing is a decidedly mixed blessing.

Once, special-interest groups could count on the support of their rank and file. Single-issue constituencies dominated politics in the 1970s, and campaigns needed to make elaborate efforts to court them. But today's well-informed voters are loath to decide whom to support based only on one issue. Special-interest groups and political-action committees (PACs) do not control the millions of votes their leaders would have us believe they do. The emperor has no clothes. The AFL-CIO, the Christian Coalition, the National Federation of Independent Businessmen (NFIB) are largely paper tigers.

Those groups whose members are such fanatics that they still vote based on a single issue (like the NRA or the Christian Coalition) are so discredited among swing voters that their support is likely to lose more votes than it picks up. The NRA, for example, is rated negatively by a margin of over 2-to-1 among American voters. A candidate under fire from this organization can usually neutralize their opposition and energize his own campaign by publicizing the fact that the NRA is attacking him, hanging their support around the neck of his opponent like a lead weight.

On the left, labor union support is often more harmful than helpful. For years, Republicans have learned to tag any liberal Democrat getting labor funds with a "union label," to his detriment at the polls.

The special-interest paper tigers like to growl and try to enforce discipline on the legislators they support. But in reality, there is little vengeance they can exact. If a candidate agrees with the basic message and philosophy of a special-interest group, he need not really worry if he doesn't jump every time the special-interest organization says so. If he is generally pro-life or pro-gun, for example, he can safely ignore the NRA or the Christian Coalition's efforts to enforce down-the-line orthodoxy. Anti-gun control Republican Tom Ridge won the Pennsylvania governorship in 1994, with strong gun-owner support, despite his heresy in backing the assault rifle ban. Bob Dole, generally pro-life, ran well among Christian Coalition voters in the Republican primaries despite his failure to toe their extreme line or win their favor in his race against their golden boy Pat Buchanan.

Generally, these organizations can only marginally affect turnout and rarely can prevail against a well-organized media campaign on behalf of the candidate they have targeted. Experts often cite the NRA's role in the congressional elections of 1994 to illustrate the power of special interests. The myth is that the NRA defeated scores of Democratic incumbents, costing Clinton control of Congress. But the dead donkeys on the field of combat in '94 were slain by their own votes for tax increases and the bumbling of the Clintons in promoting healthcare reform far more than as a result of NRA vengeance.

Special interests are so aware that they are unpopular that most publicize their support for candidates and issues through mailings to their members, since TV ads would reach more voters who hate them than who will follow their endorsements. The key in defeating special-interest groups is to use TV to publicize the role they are playing in your opponent's campaign so he pays dearly over the TV for each vote he gets through his mailings.

Special interests can generate campaign funds, but here they are basically labor-saving devices. A candidate can get just as much money—and usually more—if he works mailing lists on his own and reaches over the heads of these groups to raise money from their constituencies. He doesn't need the middleman. Indeed, when he goes through special-interest groups for money, they often force him to jump through hoops for the funds by requiring a doctrinaire loyalty that is often far more expensive at the polls than it was worth in campaign funds.

The exception to this rule is labor unions. Their money is irreplaceable because it is not given voluntarily by union members. It is extracted from them without their real approval and spent without any consultation. If labor unions could not give to political candidates, Democrats could never replace it by appealing to the individual Teamster or steelworker. It would be fun to watch the response if they tried.

Before the rapid proliferation of television news, voters tended to delegate their decisions to interest groups. Not anymore. Now, they are armed with their own sources of information and march to the beat of no drummer but that of their own ideas.

Let's take a minute to examine the main interest groups in our politics.

• *National Rifle Association:* The NRA is the most disliked of all special-interest groups among the general electorate. Knowing this, they tend to keep a low profile, using mail rather than television or radio to back or oppose candidates. In a vacuum, they are often effective. But the NRA and its extreme partisans are so unpopular that their support can be damaging among moderate voters.

• *Trial lawyers:* Increasingly, Democratic fund-raising is dominated by trial lawyer money. Never a great vote-getting organization, the lawyers are potent in the pocketbook. But a candidate whose opponent gets their largesse has only to cross the street and ask the medical societies and insurance companies for financial backing to offset his adversary's advantage. Trial lawyers are widely hated. Their ratings are at the bottom of the heap. A candidate who takes their money risks his opponents' negative ads—not usually a good trade-off.

• *The Christian Coalition:* This organization's effectiveness is overrated. There are lots of voters who will vote for or against a candidate based solely on abortion. But they make it their business to seek out this information. Their due diligence makes a formal embrace by the Christian Coalition and its allied groups largely unnecessary. Most Republicans who are generally pro-life can safely ignore the Christian Coalition by appealing over its head to the voters who make up its membership. The power of the abortion issue, particularly in Republican primaries, is huge. The power of the Christian Coalition and its leaders, per se, is relatively small.

• *Labor unions:* Empathetic with the average workingman or working woman, voters nevertheless see labor leaders as elitist, pampered, self-indulgent, and often corrupt. The day when labor leaders could deliver the votes of their members is long gone. Today, labor is a cash cow for Democratic politicians and nothing more.

But in conservative and Southern states, labor money can backfire. Voters don't object to labor support but do dislike the fact that union members have no choice or voice in who gets their money.

The public also scrutinizes the labor positions of anyone who takes union money to be sure they have not been bought off.

Lately, independent expenditures by special interests have dominated congressional election advertising. Unlimited by campaign finance laws, some groups find it to their advantage to run ads directly in a candidate's district to try to defeat his bid for reelection.

These ham-handed efforts to influence an election almost always backfire. A good political consultant will know how to use the resentment voters feel against this outside interference in order to hurt the candidate the ads seek to help. Once you use these ads to paint your adversary as the tool or puppet of special interests, these independent expenditures do the cause they support more harm than good.

In the 1996 congressional elections, the massive AFL-CIO advertising campaign which targeted Republicans backfired massively. The labor ads portrayed Republicans as savaging Medicare but failed to mention the need to balance the budget or cut taxes. With Clinton way ahead in pre-election polls, Republican consultant Arthur Finkelstein ended any hope the Democrats had of taking control of Congress by exploiting labor's extreme positions in order to win. His ads warned of the liberal agenda a Democratic president and a Democratic Congress would likely pursue. The high-profile labor intervention in the election became more of a negative issue than a positive help to Democrats and had much to do with the ultimate GOP legislative victory.

So, don't worry about defying special-interest groups—it's good for the soul and not all that bad for winning voter support.

CHAPTER 19

How to Raise Money and Keep Your Virtue

F UND-RAISING NEED NOT BE a faustian deal with the devil. A candidate can usually raise enough money to win if he aims his fund-raising at areas where he need not sell his soul for a check. All money in politics is not created equal. To keep your virtue as you pad your war chest, you must distinguish between the different types of money in politics.

People give money to candidates for five virtuous, or at least innocuous, reasons:

- They know him personally.
- They agree with his positions.
- They want to defeat the other guy.
- They want something to do that satisfies their ego.
- They back their party.

There is, of course, only one dangerous reason why people make political contributions: They want to influence the candidate after he is elected.

The way to raise enough money to win and still keep your virtue is to maximize your ability to attract money for the first five reasons so you can refuse to take money offered for venal motives. Here's how:

• *The people a candidate knows personally* give the cleanest money in politics. Usually, all they want is the thrill of knowing that their friend, school chum, drinking buddy, et cetera, is a senator. The list of people a candidate knows is almost always more numerous than he realizes. It is not just those he would invite to dinner, or even the people on his Christmas card list. A politician must range far over his life, his schoolmates, ex-boyfriends and ex-girlfriends, professional colleagues, civic- and country-club buddies and many people he might barely know in search of funds. One must climb the distant branches of one's family tree to pick fruit.

Even a hermit will find that there are thousands of people from his past who still remember him. As anyone who has become famous will agree, the number of people who suddenly claim to be personal friends is vastly greater than the number of people you actually know. A politician who does not ruthlessly exploit his past contacts in search of funds will lose either his virtue or the election—the former, by being forced to seek money that is unclean; the latter, by not seeking money at all.

• *Ideological soul mates* are also good for clean money. All they want is for you to agree with what you already believe in. Here, mere agreement suffices. Manic enthusiasm is unnecessary. If a politician has any position at all on abortion, gun control, tort reform, casino gambling, or a plethora of local issues, funds await harvest. Each side on these issues has so mobilized its constituency that a candidate can follow his conscience and still raise money from the side he agrees with. Take whatever position you want, but do take a position, because once you do, ample money awaits you on either side.

- *Those who hate one's adversary* are a particularly entertaining source of succor. Review carefully upon whom your opponent has trod and offer them a way to get even. Here, your ability to win need not play a central role. "Get even" donors will give simply to annoy and harass your opponent. In our "never turn the other cheek" society, grudges abound. The nice thing about this money is that you don't have to do anything to earn it, you just have to run against the right person.

Don't restrict your reach to those who have public-policy disagreements with your adversary. Check out the business associates he's gouged, who he's sued, who he's defamed, who he beat out in matters of the heart—anything. The money may not be given from the best of motives, but as far as you are concerned, it's clean—no payback required.

- *Ego-trippers* give money that is like manna from heaven. Like the biblical manna, it's a bit of a pain to have to collect it every day and after awhile, it all tastes the same, but it's clean money. All the donors ask is to be stroked with photos, phone calls, and personal, handwritten letters. If you remember their children's names or recall the last time you met, so much the better. When Bill Clinton let donors sleep in the Lincoln Bedroom, he was just offering them a fond memory in return for their money. It doesn't matter where your contributors sleep, it matters whether they seek to influence you when they are awake. Those docile donors who return to Des Moines to boast of their evening in the White House without stopping by to ask you for a vote or a contract or a job on the way out are the virgins of our process, to be cherished and cultivated. They are what passes for virtue in the world of political fund-raising. Fortunately, as P. T. Barnum said about them, one "is born every minute."

- *Partisans* are truly the workhorses of campaign funding. Rarely do they care who is running, they just want their side to win

a majority. They truly embody Gilbert and Sullivan's ideal of a politician: "He always voted at his party's call and he never thought of
thinking for himself at all/ He thought so little they rewarded he, by
making him the ruler of the Queen's Navee."

The key to these funds is not virtue but electability. To raise
money from a party's faithful donors, an authority figure must lay his
hands on the candidate in blessing. Over the years, party donors have
learned to watch carefully for a sign of blessing before they open
their checkbooks. When white smoke emerges from their party
committee and a candidate is anointed as "electable," they will give
generously. Once the blessing is bestowed, the compliant donors
usually have but two questions: "To whom do I make the check
payable?" and "What's the candidate's name?"

Both parties have clubs of donors—the political equivalent of
frequent-flyer programs. The Republicans, for example, have the
Eagle's Club, an association of people who pledge to donate, on
demand, $10,000 or $20,000 (or whatever is the current price of
admission) in thousand-dollar units to whichever senate or governor
candidates the party designates. Often, they are in the position of
contributing to candidates whom they've never met, don't want to
meet, and have never heard of. But they recognize that these candidates are the warm bodies who must fill the seats in Congress to give
their side a majority. Sometimes, they don't even want to be bothered
by getting a thank you note from the candidate to whom they've
donated but never heard of. Opening mail is such a chore.

How is a candidate to get the blessing of his party's leaders?
Remember Machiavelli's dictum that it is better to be feared than
loved. Rather than focus on being attractive to the party's leaders, a
candidate must be attractive to the voters instead. Those with good
poll numbers prove irresistible to king-makers, whatever their defects
or personal shortcomings.

Party leaders will inevitably huff and puff, demanding that a candidate follow their line on policy. They will want to control your strategy, decide who will be your consultants, and run your campaign for you. But feel free to tell them to go to hell. When it comes right down to it, they want fifty-one people of any shape, sex, color, or size in the Senate to vote for their candidate for Majority Leader and could care less who those fifty-one are. Don't listen to anything the party tells you. It will almost inevitably run counter to what you need to do to get elected, and if you show good poll numbers, they will fall over themselves to give you money anyway.

Because the money is so keyed to political viability, party money is usually the last to come in. A wise candidate will spend his seed money from personal acquaintances or ideological fellows on media to gain sufficient traction in polling to win the love and adoration of party oddsmakers.

Some candidates mistakenly hoard their money and slip farther back in the polls, planning to spend it all at the end. As a result, their candidacies never seem viable and the party money stays away. Even worse, some candidates spend their early seed money on staff, rent, and travel rather than on advertising. When the money is gone, the bad poll numbers remain and the candidacy dies.

• *Bad money* is that which comes with strings attached. The key is to raise enough from other sources to refuse it. It is not sufficient for a candidate to be virtuous in his heart and rely on his integrity to preserve his purity. Once you take his money, you inherit all the political baggage of your donor. Even if you don't do what the special-interest group wants, the money they gave becomes—in the public's mind—your price tag. Guilt is assumed.

Your donor list is your voting record. In 1982, Bill Clinton regained the governorship of Arkansas largely by citing his opponent's reliance on utility company funds to fuel his campaign. Republicans from Richard Nixon to Ronald Reagan have defeated Democrats from Helen Gahagan Douglas to Walter Mondale by tying them to labor funding. The most overworked cliché in politics is, "He who pays the piper calls the tune."

Every donation received is a potential negative ad. Vetting money is just as important as raising it. Has any contributor been indicted or convicted of a crime? Do any represent a special-interest anathema to the voters? Do the patterns of any donations seem suspect, suggesting fraud or that the money really is not coming from the donor but from his employer or uncle? Are any of the donors public employees who work for you or contractors who have benefited from your largesse?

Most candidates regard returning checks with the same enthusiasm that they would contemplate amputation of a limb. But the money a politician returns is worth a hundred times that amount in the cost of trying to rebut a negative ad about the donor.

Those who despair of reforming campaign finances would do well to realize that politics is usually self-correcting. So extensive has been the publicity about the evils of campaign finances that candidates must self-police to survive.

CHAPTER 20

The Myth of Media Manipulation

THE MEDIA AND THE POLITICIANS agree that newspapers and TV news are all-powerful. But they are wrong. Both believe that politicians can be very effective in manipulating what the media says. Wrong again. They are deeply convinced that the voters can be easily led by the media. Still wrong.

Policy and process are developed by the interplay of public officials, the media, and the voters. Each has its role; each has its limitations. But none of the players recognize their limits and all are constantly trying to transcend them. The key to political happiness is to accept what we cannot change and to play within the implicit ground rules of the system.

Voters live in the real world with their hopes, fears, dreams, and anxieties. But they are not very good at figuring out what to do about them. Robert Frost once wrote, "Poetry is about the grief. Politics is about the grievance."

The average public official is endowed with wealth and privilege and knows little of the quiet desperation of real people. Even if his or her childhood was traumatic, the pain is a distant memory. Most politicians wouldn't recognize a "real person" if they tripped over one.

The media plays the key role in bringing the private pains and needs of real people to public attention. Despite romantic fantasies about caring candidates who learn of America in donut shops, most politicians rely on media to teach them what concerns the average person.

But the media isn't very good at prioritizing the public's concerns or figuring out what to do about them. Despite the hubris of editorial writers, there is a good reason why they run newspapers and not nations. Most lack enough understanding of policy, budgets, programs, or politics to govern wisely. Were their editorials followed each day, the zigzag course our government would weave would leave us baffled.

So it is up to the politician to propose priorities and solutions. With the aid of polling, he is the one who has to sift through the clippings and decide upon what to focus. It is he who must come up with the answers, who must know how to translate the public's grief into the system's issues.

Once the politician has floated his issues and proposals, the media carries them to the public. But in its hubris, the media overestimates its power to move voters. News editors and reporters think that they can drive issues to the top of the list of the public's priorities. Yet, the evidence of the past few years is that the public decides on its priorities quite independently of the media. People will pay attention to what they want to, regardless of what the media thinks is important. The voters know best.

People have become terribly suspicious of the media and increasingly sophisticated in spotting its attempts at manipulation. The electorate sees the media as a kind of special-interest group, no more objective than any other in presenting its view. Like the readers of *Pravda* in the former Soviet Union, voters are increasingly selective in which stories they believe and which they discount.

When voters are determined to ignore a story, they do so with grit and determination despite the efforts of the media to interest them. Consider the case of Rwanda. Never has there been a story the media wanted to cover more, nor one about which the public wished less to hear. For years, every night's news carried horrific footage of maimed babies, raped women, and dead men. But the public didn't care. Yet the media hammered away, rightly considering it a moral duty to bring this suffering to the conscience of America. But the public still had no tolerance for American intervention. The television coverage did nothing to spur popular demand for military involvement.

The massive coverage of scandal in the Clinton administration and its minimal impact on the elections of 1996 or 1998 is another good case in point. In June of 1996, half of all television news shows riveted on the FBI file scandal. To listen to the news, one would have assumed that Clinton was on his way out. But Clinton's lead over Dole dropped by only three points despite all the pounding, and he quickly restored those points the next month. In 1998, the Lewinsky scandal had no impact on Democratic candidates throughout the country.

On the other hand, the public is diligent in searching out news it does care about. Even when the media is determined to underplay, distort, or ignore the message a politician is putting out, if the issue works, it will reach the voters.

President Clinton issues almost daily messages through press conferences, media events, and speeches to suggest measures aimed at meeting the needs of America's families in their daily lives. Each day, Clinton speaks out on topics like teen smoking, drunk driving, school construction, educational standards, college scholarships, guns in schools, TV violence and sexual content, computers in classrooms, cell phones for community watch groups, and school uniforms and curfews.

The media constantly belittles these initiatives as "bite-sized" and laments the absence of bold, sweeping presidential vision.

When the media covers his statements, it is through a veil of criticism, calling the ideas "small-bore," "opportunistic," and "unpresidential."

But the voters seek out the ideas they want and read the president's statements, ignoring the media's criticism. Day after day, these "small-bore" ideas have held up the president's popularity, demonstrating his connection to the problems of the average person despite the daily pounding of scandal and congressional hearings.

If the media overstates its power in shaping public opinion, politicians and their "spin doctors" overstate their ability to influence the media. A politician can have very little impact over how he is covered or presented. The media will cover his ideas as it wishes. It will give them the headlines, the placement, the slant, the photos, and the play it chooses. At most, politicians can influence the process around the edges. The vast bulk of the time public officials, candidates, and their staffs spend on spinning the news is largely ineffective, mostly irrelevant, and basically unnecessary.

It is ironic that political consultants and handlers are called "spin doctors" and that much of the media coverage they receive revolves around their effectivness at manipulating the media. This characterization is founded on a mutually reinforcing conceit. Consultants and press secretaries overly pride themselves on their ability to manipulate press coverage, which they really can't. The media revels in the assumption that its slant and bias are so important that they are worthy of the skills of great manipulators, which they really aren't.

Politicians and their handlers overstate their influence on the media. President Clinton's ability to recover, so far, from the scandals that have plagued his administration is, at the time of this writing, extraordinary. Hubristic consultants and spin doctors have taken full credit for his nine lives by extolling their ability to structure media coverage of the president's accusers.

But polling shows that most of America believes that private matters should remain private. It is not the skill of the president's staff in deflecting blame that is keeping his ratings afloat. Voters are much more independent than media experts want to believe.

In other administrations also, handlers have overstated their ability to control events. Despite all the efforts of Reagan's people, few voters believed the president was ignorant of the arms-for-hostages trade. The manipulations of Bush's media advisors did nothing to convince voters that the president was on the job fighting the recession day and night. And all the queen's horses and all the queen's men and women could not hold Hillary's healthcare package together.

An issue will stand or fall on its own merits based on the real-life experience of voters and their innate ability to distinguish the real from the phony, the practical from the illusory.

The job of a consultant or handler is to help a candidate or public official find a place to stand from which to move the earth. Once they find the proper ground, this "great huge world will come round to them," in Emerson's words.

So, there is good news and bad news for the politician. The bad news is that his staff can have little influence over how his ideas are presented by the media. But here is the good news it doesn't really matter. The public reserves to itself the right to decide what to accept and what to reject. The slant and bias of the media does little to influence their decisions; it is overwhelmingly the content of the ideas that matters.

Everybody thinks they have more influence than they do in this process. So, a few basic principles should guide our understanding of the interplay of voters, the media, and politicians.

• Politicians are not very good at understanding what people want and need. The media has to explain it to them.

• The media fails to prioritize the problems it covers or to develop solutions. Politicians are much better at developing answers, and voters do their own prioritization regardless of the media's attempts to manipulate them.

• Political handlers are largely unsuccessful in affecting how stories are covered. The media usually does just what it pleases. There may be an episodic victory in structuring the coverage of one outlet or one reporter, but the pluralism of the media and its multiplicity of outlets make real success at spin beyond reach.

• Voters don't much care what the media thinks. They peer past the editorials, the headlines, and even past the front page to find out what they want to know and to get answers to the problems they consider important. No matter how little coverage a story gets or how slanted it is, voters will draw their own conclusions.

With due regard for the difficulties in manipulating media coverage, there are certain ideas that might help a politician maximize such opportunities as he does have to influence it.

The most important part of selling a story is the sound bite. The rest of the statement can be boilerplate or detail. It is the one-paragraph sound bite on which the story lives or dies. The better the quote, the more likely it is to make its way into print and the more likely it is to shape the story. Style matters. Some sound bites, like Clinton's "The era of big government is over," or Reagan's "Government is the problem, not the solution," define an entire philosophy, not just that day's news.

But the most delicate of tasks is developing the analytic line of the day. In the Clinton administration, presidential aide George Stephanopoulos and Press Secretary Mike McCurry would carefully analyze the mood of the media and seek to galvanize it into a "spin" that would dominate the news analysis. They did it well because they approached the task with humility. They realized they had to work with the existing preconceptions of the media and were able, at best, to alter them only slightly or to channel them in the direction they wanted. But only slightly. They both realized that you couldn't bring about 180-degree, 90-degree, or even 45-degree turns. Their slant and spin was based on a profound understanding of what reporters are thinking and a sensitive ability to predict how they will react to suggestions. Senator Eugene McCarthy trenchantly noted that the press were like blackbirds on a telephone wire. When one took off, all the others followed. If you can get a few top reporters to see the news from your angle, it will spread rapidly down the line.

Humility is especially important when reporters call with their own stories. Remember that reporters usually have written the story in their mind before they start. They formulate a hypothesis and then gather evidence to prove it right or wrong. Rarely do they cast a wide net and inductively seek to find a pattern while keeping a completely open mind. Their original hypothesis will most likely be the story's final verdict.

A reporter usually begins his call by laying out his thesis. Live within it. Don't try to change it. See if you can steer the story within the parameters of what the reporter wants to write anyway.

When the press was working on the story of what motivated Clinton to seek NATO expansion, the mind-set of the press was that Clinton wanted to get votes in the white ethnic neighborhoods in the Midwest. In fact, this consideration was very remote in the president's thinking, not that he's above it; he just doesn't believe that white ethnic divisions are that important in the Midwest. He expanded NATO because he is haunted by Richard Nixon's question from the grave: "Who lost Russia? Who lost Eastern Europe?" But the press would not be deflected. The best Clinton's press handlers could do was to sell the idea that politics affected the timing of Clinton's discussion of the issue (before the election) but had not been his motive in making the decision itself.

Reporters will write the story they want to write. All evidence is either helpful—and gets included—or is unhelpful and is omitted or downplayed. It's their paper. They do what they want.

When you see a negative story coming, go through the motions of rebuttal but understand that the only way to come out ahead is to distract attention from the piece by making some other news that is more compelling. When David Maraniss wrote his biography of Clinton, *First in His Class*, exposing more of his sexual past, the president chose the moment of its release to intervene in the baseball strike. He knew that he didn't have any leverage to exact a settlement and that owners and players were too far gone to listen to reason. He knew he'd fail. But the baseball strike story was a whole lot better than letting the Maraniss book dominate the weekend's coverage.

When David Stockman, President Reagan's budget director, told a reporter that he realized early on that supply-side economics would swell, not reduce, the deficit—even though he had said the opposite at the time in public—all hell broke loose. The liberal media jumped all over the Stockman quote, attacking his cynicism in backing tax cuts that he apparently knew would balloon the deficit while preaching deficit reduction.

Reagan's people deflected the story by describing in lurid detail how Stockman was punished for his remarks. In a famous quote, they told the media that the president had "taken David to the woodshed" to express his anger. By focusing on the punishment—and on whether Reagan would fire Stockman—they deflected the central negative thrust of the story.

In handling television, bear in mind that the medium cannot help itself. It needs pretty pictures. Even if you feel that only misanthropes write the copy for the evening news, remember that those who choose the visuals for the story want attractive footage. If you frame a good-looking visual, it will make it past the editors and go out over the air. Caught between negative reporters and artistic film editors, TV news programs are often a civil war between the text and the visual. The text is up to them. The visual is up to you.

Backdrops matter. The candidate should stand in front of an assemblage of American flags or a bevy of uniformed police with medals. Right over his head, so it has to make it into the cameraman's shot, should be a printed message summarizing the theme of the statement. Slogans like "Creating Jobs," "Raising Education Standards," or "Protecting the Environment" should blare their message on the TV screen. That way, even if the TV editor cuts out your candidate's voice and superimposes a soundtrack of an anchorman or reporter dumping on your candidate, the message du jour will still come through.

Many observers, particularly on the right, impute an ideological bias to the press. On the other hand, President Clinton never thought the media was tilted to the left. He felt it was focused on opportunism and careerism with each individual reporter hunting for a scalp and a prize regardless of the facts. I think both analyses miss the point.

Mark Hertsgaard's excellent book about the coverage of the Reagan presidency, *On Bended Knee*, assigns the key role in determining media bias to institutional history. Tracing the oscillations of relations between the press and the presidency, Hertsgaard notes that the media was chagrined by its intimacy with President Kennedy and revolted by its credulity in accepting Johnson's version of the facts at face value during the Vietnam War. Their ensuing anger at their own failures made them overreact when Richard Nixon took office. An especially attractive target, he helped journalists compensate for their past complacency in covering the White House. But when the anger at Nixon spilled over into negative coverage of Ford and Carter, the media wondered if it was not permanently condemning America to one-term, ineffective presidents by its acerbic tone and jaundiced attitude. Hertsgaard says that President Reagan benefited from journalist guilt over their past excesses and enjoyed comparative media largesse as a result. To carry this analysis forward, one would have to assume that President Clinton has been the unwilling victim of the media's self-criticism over its indulgent attitude toward Reagan and Bush.

This kind of media mood swing is far more likely than either ideology or blind ambition to motivate press coverage. But the public understands the moods of its journalists and will ignore both incessantly negative and constantly positive coverage to seek out what it wants.

CHAPTER 21

How to Survive a Scandal

THERE IS NO WAY TO "WIN" at scandal coverage. The only way to come out alive is to tell the truth, take the hit, and move on. Then you need to distract public attention from the scandal by focusing on other, larger items in your agenda.

When a scandal breaks, the chances are that the reporter writing the story has his ammunition all lined up for the next few days. He and his editors deliberately parcel out the story, piece by piece, to be sure that each day a new "revelation" confirms the idea that the scandal is spreading. News organizations have to allocate so many financial and personnel resources to leading the way on a scandal, they must sell the importance of the issue with all their might.

In that sense, each scandal has a journalistic parent. The *Washington Post*, of course, fathered the Watergate scandal. It was the *New York Times* that developed the Whitewater affair. The *Post* controlled the play on the Chinese campaign contributions scandal.

Since each journalistic parent protects its offspring, to counter a scandal in the pages of the paper that originated it is an inevitably flawed strategy. The journalistic "owner" of the scandal has lined up his facts with far greater care than any haphazard defense can rebut.

The key in limiting the damage of a scandal is not to lie. It is rarely the scandal that gets you; it's the lying. One lie leads to another, and soon what was an embarrassment comes to border on a criminal obstruction of justice. Politicians who are wary of taking their medicine when a scandal breaks and seek to dodge responsibility by not telling the truth are only digging a deeper hole for themselves.

When the Lewinsky scandal broke in the press, President Clinton called me to ask for advice. I urged him to consider telling the truth, citing how Nixon had dug his own grave by piling falsehood and cover-ups on top of each other. Intrigued, he agreed that I should conduct a survey to see how voters would react to the news that he had had an affair with a twenty-two-year-old intern. The poll suggested that while the public would forgive the sex, they would not forgive the perjury. By lying in his deposition in the Paula Jones case weeks before, the president had made an immediate admission of fault impossible.

Even so, he waited far too long to come clean (and, in my opinion, has not done so at the time of this writing). His failure to absorb political embarrassment and personal pain by telling the truth made a big scandal into a potentially lethal one.

Ultimately, it takes personal courage to step up and admit blame, accepting responsibility for wrongdoing. Cowards hide behind lies, and they make the scandal worse by doing so.

But the weakness of any scandal is its political salience. While the law and our supposed moral code speak in absolutes of right and wrong, people live in the real world and understand the shadings of gray. They are unwilling to defrock a public figure just because it is alleged that a rigid line has been crossed and a law broken. They have seen too many good men fall because of technical infractions and watched bad men triumph because they acted legally, if unethically and immorally.

In fact, most voters are reluctant ever to oust a public figure over scandal alone. No president, and very few governors, senators, or congressmen, have ever been denied reelection because of scandal. The electorate, in effect, sees a clear division between its duty to elect people who reflect its ideals and public-policy convictions, and the system's duty to assure that wrongdoers are punished. The voters are saying that if an accuser can prove the facts of a scandal, let the public official be ousted, but until he does, leave him alone. The elected official must play to this larger sense of society's interests by continuing to govern with vision and foresight even amid the crossfire of scandal.

In weathering scandal, it is important to look closely at the ultimate public reaction to what you are accused of doing. If voters would be truly outraged at what they say you did, you better not have done it. Stealing money is not often forgiven. But in many scandals, voters are willing to cut you slack even if the press and your political opponents are not. Voters were forgiving over the Clinton sex scandals, the travel office firings, and the Iran-Contra affair. The politicians of the other party were outraged, but the voters weren't particularly exercised. By playing the vitriol of your adversaries against the tolerance of your electorate, you can defeat many scandals. Voters are likely to see the accuser as guilty of partisanship and a personal grudge rather than accuse you of malfeasance.

Where moral scandals are concerned, Americans currently fall into three categories, largely along generational lines. Older voters tend to be socially conservative and harshly judgmental. They see conduct in terms of absolutes and are unforgiving. They are usually irredeemably lost when a public figure faces scandal. Baby boomers tend to be morally relativistic and are less likely to condemn public figures for sex, drugs, or other lifestyle scandals. Generation Xers, voters now in their twenties and thirties, are conservative and do not condone immorality in their public officials. But they are far too concerned with the daily duty of raising their own children to worry much about the moral behavior of the president. For these voters, the key is not the president's character, but his actions—do they make it easier to raise children properly?

The Clinton political team of 1996 used, as a guide, the idea that "public values offset private scandal." By speaking up on issues like teen tobacco use, drugs, drunk driving, gun control, education standards, family leave, health coverage, and the like, Clinton regained the loyalty of the Generation X voters who had been turned off by his omnipresent scandals.

Clinton's political focus on values issues developed in early 1995 when polls showed that he was winning the votes of single people, breaking even among those who were married and childless, and losing among people who were married and lived with children. Clinton's failure among the latter group was directly related to questions about his morality and character as a result of the daily pounding of scandal. By pushing a public-values agenda, Clinton was able to move ahead among married voters with children despite their continuing doubts about Clinton's character.

In fighting scandal, the key is not to overreact. President Nixon was not undone by criticism of his war policies. He was destroyed by his overreaction to the criticism. It was his attempts to wiretap reporters, break into the offices of Daniel Ellsberg's psychiatrist in search of damaging material, and burglarize Democratic headquarters that led to his resignation.

When scandal comes, presidents are tempted to rely on secret detectives who will dig up dirt on potential opponents and witnesses. Off-the-shelf operatives always seem to have the answers. In the 1992 campaign, former Clinton Chief of Staff Betsey Wright oversaw the operations of detective Jack Palladino. In 1992, the *Washington Post* reported that Palladino was digging up negative information on women who were rumored to have had sexual affairs with Bill Clinton, with the intent either of discrediting them should they go public with accusations or of cowing them into silence. Directly and through an attorney, the gumshoe got $118,000, including federal matching funds.

It is exactly this sort of overreaction that can kill a candidate or a president.

At the time of this writing, President Clinton has just survived a Senate impeachment trial, not over illicit sex, but over how he handled the scandal. His failure to tell the truth and his desperate efforts to cover his tracks were the basis of the allegations against him.

Most scandals are not so lethal that they need this kind of a defense. The public is broadly tolerant and knows that nobody would be completely clean if their every move, every tax return, every sexual involvement were held up to the light of public scrutiny. Presidents and elected officials at all levels need to trust the sense and perspective of the American people, not the scorched-earth tactics of counterinvestigation and witness intimidation.

The best way to survive a scandal is to let the chips fall where they may and trust the people while doing all you can to make yourself indispensable in the office you hold.

The Key Danger: Personality Change

P RESIDENTS SOON FIND that their vision is clouded by a kind of fog that surrounds them. Like most fog, it is caused by a cold front colliding with a warm front. In the case of the White House, the cold front is the icy criticism, cynicism, and vilification to which most presidents are subjected. The warm front is the obsequious flattery that surrounds the president in every corner of the White House and comes from every member of his staff.

When criticism from the outside collides with adulation from the inside, the result is a kind of fog, which beclouds presidential vision. Some presidents are permanently altered by this fog. In some, bitterness, paranoia, and defensiveness overcome their personalities and cripple them as people and as presidents.

The unreal environment of the American presidency can permanently alter all but the most grounded of men or women. The constant security, the mass of servants, the legions of flatterers, and the natural tendency to respond to criticism by drawing closer to those who fawn can change a person beyond recognition. Likely the single greatest danger any president faces is the prospect of a personality change as he soaks in the adoration of those who eat his bread and sing his praises.

History reflects just this kind of personality change in failed presidencies. President Ulysses S. Grant went from a soldier in a tent to a consort of magnates and let them steal the country blind all around him (without getting anything for himself). President Woodrow Wilson went from an astute reformer, skilled at sensing popular changes and catching their wind, to an isolated, brittle, and inflexible moralist as he campaigned for his League of Nations. Herbert Hoover morphed from a dedicated humanitarian feeding millions to an isolated, bankerish aristocrat hidden behind the walls of the presidency. Lyndon Johnson wallowed ever deeper in self-pity until he began to see his own countrymen as adversaries. Once the paternalistic savior of civil rights and poverty, he became an isolated, embattled, and embittered leader. Richard Nixon's demons took over from his common sense as he felt surrounded, vilified, and misunderstood by the liberal media establishment. Woodrow Wilson, Herbert Hoover, Lyndon Johnson, and Richard Nixon all fell prey to the personality distortions that are caused by constant and ongoing exposure to extreme praise from some and extreme criticism from others.

Secure, well-grounded personalities seem to cope better with the presidential environment. Theodore Roosevelt was so imbued with the excitement of the job that it likely never occurred to him to step back and care about the flattery he received from some and the damnation from others. The former was his due and the latter his challenge to overcome. But both were bully good fun.

Franklin Roosevelt's inner sense, perhaps developed out of his long personal ordeal, seemed never to be scathed by outside events. Only when his 1937 attempt to pack the Supreme Court with new justices failed did he seem to lose his joy and acquire the mask of the persecuted. Even under the strain of ill health and relative old age, he remained what he had called Al Smith in his nominating speech at the 1928 Democratic National Convention—the Happy Warrior.

Harry Truman's feisty contempt for all critics, and his remarkable self-possession, seemed to suggest that he didn't much care what his opponents said about him. One can imagine the obscenities with which he likely dismissed his detractors. His victory in 1948, against all predictions, seems to have reinforced this "I could care less what you think" attitude which served as his own personal insulation against paranoia and bitterness.

Eisenhower descended to the presidency from an even more important challenge earlier in his life, when he commanded the Allied forces in Europe during World War II. No decision he ever made as president likely took the same toll on his psyche as the judgment to land on D-day against overwhelming odds. He alone, perhaps, entered the presidency equipped to cope with its special strains on one's personality.

For Ronald Reagan, one gets the sense that he played the role of president and tended to attribute the criticism he received to the character he played, not to his inner persona. The character called for a friendly, open approach and Reagan played it perfectly, as he was professionally trained to do. Just as the show must go on and an actor must leave his blues in the dressing room, so it seems that Reagan's studied cheerfulness carried him through his years onstage. Likely he developed the same team approach to his presidency that he had adopted toward the films in which he starred. Rising or falling together, he didn't take personally the criticism leveled at his films by the reviewers. Let the critics pound the script, the director, the producer, or the other actors. Why would it concern him? After all, he only played the lead.

George Bush, the son of a senator, born to the purple, seems to have been equipped by heredity and background to cope with "the sort of thing" one endures as president. Like a hereditary monarch or a born aristocrat, he seemed accustomed to the unique circumstances of presidential life and insulated against bitterness by a noblesse oblige attitude inculcated from birth. What his heredity did not prepare him for, decades and decades of personal experience at the side of three presidents did. He floated above reproach and took his lumps in stride. While he reportedly became despondent after his defeat, there is no record of paranoia or bitter reproach, just eternal grace and charm in the face of adversity.

Each successful president needs a personal strategy to avoid changing in office. He must map out a way to steer clear of the paranoia, grandiosity, and self-pity that seem to be the hallmarks of a ruined presidency. Above all, a president must enter office with a strong center of gravity and must keep it forceful and intact. He needs the ballast of a strong spirituality and familial grounding, lest he be buffeted by the waves of criticism and adoration that pound on his soul.

In President Clinton's case, a deep pragmatic insecurity about his political standing, born of his frequent bouts with electoral adversity, keeps him from becoming arrogant amid flattery. His antennae for those who dislike him is so acute that he will single them out of a crowd and focus all his energies on winning over his single critic in a room. With an almost deaf ear to praise, he picks up the slightest vibration of criticism and lets it resonate at his core.

For President Clinton, the haunting memory of how quickly the pomp went away after his 1980 defeat for reelection, after just two years tasting the good life as governor of Arkansas, inoculates him from internalizing the adulation with which he is surrounded. Criticism, too, usually leaves Clinton unchanged. Being his own harshest critic, he usually leaps to all the negative conclusions others voice long before they even find out about the shortcoming.

The more one evaluates the possibilities for personality change in the White House, the more the dichotomy elaborated by James David Barber in his book, *Presidential Character*, appears relevant. Writing in 1972, and doubtless suffering a hangover from the Johnson and Nixon days, Barber says the possibility of a president turning sullen and paranoid is related to whether or not he likes the job.

Does he seem to experience his political life as happy or sad, enjoyable or discouraging, positive or negative in its main effect? What I am after here is not grim satisfaction in a job well done, not some philosophical conclusion. The idea is this: Is he someone who, on the surfaces we can see, gives forth the feeling that he has fun in his political life? Whether a man is burdened by power or enjoys power, whether he is trapped by responsibility or made free by it, whether he is moved by other people and outer forces or moves them—that is the essence of leadership. By Barber's standard, FDR, Theodore Roosevelt, Harry Truman, Ronald Reagan, and Bill Clinton would all be positive personalities, relatively resistant to the change in temperament that negative developments so often bring. Lyndon Johnson, Richard Nixon, and Herbert Hoover would be most vulnerable to a change in attitude and, eventually, in personality as their administrations progressed.

A president would do well to remember two stanzas from Rudyard Kipling's poem "If":

If you can dream—and not make dreams your master;
If you can think—and not make thoughts your aim;
If you can meet with triumph and disaster
And treat those two imposters just the same;

If you can talk with crowds and keep your virtue;
And walk with kings—nor lose the common touch;
If neither foes nor loving friends can hurt you;
If all men count with you, but none too much . . .

How to Get Your Staff to Do What You Want

WHEN PRESIDENT HARRY S. TRUMAN pondered how well his successor, General Dwight David Eisenhower, would do in the Oval Office, he shook his head sadly. "He'll say 'do this' and 'do that' and nothing will happen. It's not like the military."

Even though a president appoints his staff and can generally fire them at will, it is very hard to get them to do what you want them to do, and even harder to stop them from manipulating you.

One reason for the independence of staff is that very few elected officials are entirely free to appoint whomever they choose to staff jobs. Some people have to be appointed to appease political factions or interest groups the politician needs to cultivate. Sometimes, a major financial donor or political leader, called a "rabbi" in the street parlance of ward politics, pushes a person for a staff job. Frequently, a staff position is really an ambassadorship or a liaison between a vital interest group or demographic block and the politician. This divided loyalty makes it all the more difficult to enforce your will on your staff.

Presidents from Abe Lincoln to Bill Clinton have chosen staffs made up of ambassadors to the various factions of their party. As President Lyndon Johnson said, earthily, "I'd rather have him inside the tent pissing out than outside the tent pissing in."

Lincoln's cabinet included virtually every one of his defeated rivals for the Republican presidential nomination. As the party's second candidate for president, Lincoln felt acutely the need to include in his cabinet those who he needed in his governing coalition. Secretary of State William Seward had been the front runner for the 1860 nomination before the convention deadlocked. Secretary of the Treasury Salmon P. Chase and Secretary of War Edwin M. Stanton had also both been convention rivals. Montgomery Blair, the postmaster general, and Simeon Cameron, the ambassador to Russia (after a short, unhappy stint as war secretary) were both emissaries from the party organizations in Maryland and Pennsylvania respectively. Lincoln's cabinet resembled a British cabinet, bring together all the leaders of his party, than an American cabinet, which is intended to be a group of advisors to the president.

President Clinton's choice of his cabinet and staff reflected the same need Lincoln had, to include all the diverse members of his governing coalition. He had to be sure African-Americans were represented in his cabinet and staff, so he reached out for Mississippi congressman Mike Espy, whom he barely knew, to serve as Secretary of Agriculture. To represent labor, Clinton named Harold Ickes, a former union lawyer, as his deputy chief of staff. The Democratic barons in the House had their man, former congressman Leon Panetta, first as director of the Office of Management and Budget and then as chief of staff. House Democratic Speaker Dick Gephardt saw his own former staff member, George Stephanopoulos, enter the president's inner circle. Senate Democratic leader Tom Daschle's former chief of staff, John Hilley, became the president's director of congressional relations.

Of President Clinton's inner staff and cabinet, only a handful of people could be said to have been part of his inner circle in Arkansas. Most of these were quickly shunted aside. Mac MacLarty, the president's childhood friend, lasted only halfway through the first term as chief of staff before the Washington insiders forced the president to turn to Panetta. David Watkins, Webb Hubbell, David Kennedy, Vince Foster, Bernie Nussbaum, and most other Clinton friends were out by the middle of the first term. Thereafter, Clinton had to govern with a staff that was essentially composed of strangers and recent acquaintances.

Once, cabinets and staffs had to be balanced geographically. Now, they have to be balanced ethnically and demographically (as President Clinton said, his cabinet needed to "look like America"). Now, in addition, they must include all the relevant wings of one's party. By the time a president (or any other executive officer) finishes taking account of these various considerations, he may or may not have a good cabinet or staff. But certainly he probably doesn't have a loyal one.

So a chief executive must resort to psychology to enforce his will on his staff. In the movie version of the book *Primary Colors*, Governor Stanton's (Clinton's) longtime aide and anti-negative ad bodyguard Libby Holden looks up at the moon, right before she kills herself, and says that those who work for Stanton and his wife reflect their light. "God, they were so good and glowing, I could go for years without remembering I wasn't producing any warmth myself, any *light* of my own, . . . Without them, I'm dark and black and cold and dead and empty and airless for eternity. . . . All they need is to *glow.*"

The staff of a president is made up of moons, with no illumination of their own. Only by positioning themselves to catch the rays of the sun can they attract any attention at all. To control his staff, a president needs to aim his rays where he wants his staff to be so that they have to go there in order to catch them.

A staff member's power is the most fluid thing in politics. The White House is a monarchy much like the court of Louis XIV. When the king smiled on one of the courtiers, word rippled through Versailles at the speed of sound. Likewise, a frown is seen halfway around the beltway in an instant. Like anxious children, staff members soon learn what pleases the president-father. The chief executive has only to beam his pleasure at a staffer and the minion will hasten to earn more smiles by repeating the behavior that has won him approval and favor.

A good chief executive uses his weapons of praise and blame to cultivate diversity in the input from his staff. No president can know, in advance, which strategy will work. He needs to be sure to get a pluralistic range of inputs so that he can test each and find which are most successful.

By trying a bit of everything, empirically, and testing through polling how it's going over, a president can usually stumble on the right answer. One doubts that FDR knew in advance the impact of his fireside chats. The historical record reflects how Harry Truman, at the urging of Clark Clifford, happened upon his extemporaneous style of speaking. The televised Kennedy press conference was clearly a breakthrough, but few would have known, before it was tried, how uniquely effective it would be in showing America JFK's wit and mental acuity. Perhaps only Ronald Reagan and his staff, so schooled in the ways of Hollywood, really knew beforehand how potent their chosen means of communication—the preframed media event—would be.

Certainly the Clinton White House arrived at its bite-sized "issue du jour" communications strategy through trial and error. Since the Republican Congress balked at passing any presidential initiative, Clinton decided that this one-issue-a-day focus gave him the ability to communicate a sense of accomplishment even in the face of an intransigent Congress.

A president needs to follow FDR's advice (frequently repeated by Clinton) and use "bold, persistent experimentation" to find a tactical pattern of communications that works well. Once he's found it, he needs to steer his staff to it by his reflected approval or discontent. He must apply his smiles and frowns judiciously to bring to the fore the behavior he wants from his people.

A president, or likely any executive, needs to work hard to figure out who is really giving him good advice. With four hundred members of the White House staff and thousands more in the agencies, it takes a detective to locate who originated a good idea. As John Kennedy said, "Success has a thousand fathers but failure is an orphan." It takes an elaborate system of spies and informants to keep a president abreast of who wrote the speech he is about to give, who came up with the policy ideas, and who scheduled the event. A president needs to hunt through the bureaucracy to find the staff people who are really giving him good advice. John Kennedy's style of interaction with staff is probably the best way to do it, but with the extensive trappings of the modern-day presidency, it is hard to imagine a president roaming the corridors of the Executive Office Building, sticking his nose in each office unobtrusively and asking what each person is doing.

Instead, the president needs to look with suspicion at his generals and with interest at his junior officers to find out who is producing for him. The resulting battlefield promotions, made in the heat of reality, not in the cool planning process before the inauguration, often provide the most loyal and effective staff.

There is nothing simple about managing the staff at the White House. Direct orders usually find their way into the newspapers. Memos become embarrassing leaks. Idle comments at meetings become front-page stories. A skilled president doesn't give direct orders. He uses the alternation of praise and blame to get what he wants.

CHAPTER 24

How to Keep Your Staff
from Controlling You

THE OFFICIAL AT THE TOP of the pyramid of executive power is the one who has to stand or fall on his own merits. On election day, it is he who must command a majority. In history, it is he who will be judged. Today's electorate demands performance and is impatient with failure. To succeed at appeasing voters who demand their will be done, a political leader must master his staff and make it march to his own beat.

A politician's staff, particularly a president's staff, will always try to maximize its power. Without clear job definitions and with all power flowing from the man at the top, staff members constantly work to expand their area of jurisdiction and control. Invariably, this power diminishes the options, flexibility, and power of the president himself. Like it or not, in politics there is always a subtle struggle for control between an executive and his staff.

In the Clinton White House, a genuine terror gripped much of the staff when the president went out on what they regarded as an uncharted course (i.e., one they hadn't planned for him). "He's freelancing," they would complain derisively, almost as if they were saying the president had escaped his shackles. Their anxiety suggested that they felt that "he's loose."

The basis of the power of staff members is that they can't be fired. Few politicians can countenance a bloody trail of angry, disgruntled former aides spilling their guts to the newspapers. In times past, before investigations and special prosecutors were a fact of life, irritable presidents like Lyndon Johnson could fire people at will. But no more; a public official's staff today could well be his accusers, or at least his detractors, tomorrow.

President Clinton once gloated privately that he had succeeded in getting a person he suspected of habitual leaking to the press—David Dryer—transferred out of the White House. "I worked at it for months," the president said. "I kept raising it with Leon [Panetta, the chief of staff] and finally I got it done. He's out of here." The president of the United States, who has the legal right to rule the appointed staff of the executive branch like a king, was overjoyed that he had managed to transfer—not to terminate, but to transfer—someone he had so disliked that he had been working to get rid of him for months.

President Clinton was, literally, terrified to fire anybody. With the hailstorm of scrutiny, criticism, and investigation to which he had been subject, he simply could not afford to make any employee mad at him. In fact, there is virtually no record of Clinton firing anybody except under pressure of scandal.

For White House staff members, their access to information guarantees their tenure in office. Dismissal is a legal right a modern president can't exercise. Armed with job security, staff members do their best to fence in a president. Their arsenal of weapons is formidable.

• *Leaking to the press.* Almost every White House staffer has his or her favorite reporter. Everyone knows who feeds whom. Once, the president asked angrily how a certain piece of information about his polls got into the press. When he learned that the polls had gone to George Stephanopoulos and Rahm Emanuel, two top Clinton aides, the president shouted incredulously, "You *only* told George and Rahm? You only told George and Rahm? Why didn't you just issue a press release?" Later, when Emanuel curbed his leaking habits, Clinton noted with satisfaction, "he's our leaker now."

Leaks to the press are meant to deny the president maneuvering room or to foreclose his options. After President Clinton had decided to grant Wisconsin a waiver to reform its welfare law, liberal staff members from the Department of Health and Human Services leaked to the *New York Times* that he was planning to deny the state's request. They had no basis for the story. They just wanted to fence Clinton in with the leak.

How do you stop a leaker? Use the Leon Panetta method. Clinton's chief of staff in the second half of his first term virtually eliminated hostile leaks from the White House. He kept careful track of leaks and tried to figure out who had leaked what. Did the reporter praise a certain staff member in a profile a month after the leak appeared? Did the view expressed in the leak parallel something a staff member had been saying in private? Which reporters regularly quoted which staffers in their stories? Each question led to an evidentiary trail that helped him to figure out who was leaking.

When Leon had decided who was guilty, he would retaliate in the best possible way—a counterleak. A story would appear in the *Wall Street Journal,* one of his favored organs, reporting anonymously that one staffer or another was "losing influence" or "on his way out" or "on the president's bad side." It wouldn't be true, but it did serve to hurt the presumed leaker. Leon would always deny that he had anything to do with the counterleak and would usually shake his head in dismay at its appearance. But staff people got the point.

To leak to the press was to be discredited in the press. The empire struck back.

Leon's court was a secret one and the evidence often didn't measure up. Probably a lot of innocent people got hurt. But most of the guilty ones were hurt as well. And the leaking stopped.

• *Scheduling.* The White House equivalent of keeping the president "barefoot and pregnant" is to overschedule him. On the plane, away from Washington, the president can't communicate freely with the outside world. There is always the danger of phone calls from Air Force One being overheard. Of course, sensitive matters of national security can be discussed on secure phones, but equally sensitive political conversations can't be held without risking a leak that the president is using national security equipment for political purposes. In addition, the people who connect the calls could be leaking. People in nearby seats on Air Force One can often overhear what is said as the caller shouts to be heard above the roar of jet engines. All these factors make it hard for the president to communicate with the outside world while on board his plane.

By contrast, the staff on Air Force One has the president close at hand—much more than they do when his secretary is on duty guarding the entrance to the Oval Office. When the president travels, he is the captive of his traveling companions. White House staff love to send the president on trips because it makes him that much easier to control.

Exhaustion is another favorite staff tactic in dominating a president. Schedule him until he can't see straight and needs a few days to sleep off the trip and the time zones. That way, he won't be there, effectively, to supervise you.

President Clinton was completely convinced that his staff used these techniques to control him. In 1997, he noted that he had made progress in forcing his staff to do what he wanted. "They still try to pull the usual stuff about overscheduling me and tiring me out, but I've cut it way back," he said.

A president, or any executive in politics, needs to understand that his desire to move around his state or nation undermines his ability to lead effectively. The more he moves his body, the less he can use his mind. He needs to keep a tight rein on his travel and spend as much time as possible at his desk running the office. The White House will run itself when the president is away. That's why he has to be sure not to be away very much.

• *Information flow and options.* The favorite technique of military and diplomatic advisors is to restrict the flow of information to the president and to pose options in decision memos that are stacked in favor of their point of view. Repeatedly, President Clinton expressed frustration with the limited options he got from his staff. A chief executive is just too busy to formulate his own list of alternative courses he might take. He can't reach out and check the practicality of new ideas that occur to him. He's dependent on the staff to do the checking.

The word "can't" is a favorite at the White House—the most powerful building in the world. "You can't, Mr. President," is everybody's most frequent line. Lawyers say he can't because of constitutional objections. Foreign policy people say he can't due to diplomatic complications. Military experts say he can't because of technical considerations. The political people say he can't because of pressure from the party. The congressional relations people say he can't because the Congress will "go ballistic."

Can't, can't, can't.

But a president can. All he needs to do is to understand that he must bypass his formal, paid staff with a part-time "kitchen cabinet" of outside advisors who work for him in fact but not in name. For every area of presidential focus, he needs non-governmental people to feed him information and options. They'll do it gladly for a president—even for free and without credit—and they will arm the chief executive to fight the straitjacket his staff would impose on him. Unless a president has a network of outside advisors, he will be trapped, bound, and shackled by his own inside experts.

Every president must remember that he is locked in a zero-sum game with his staff. The more power he has, the less they have. The more they seize, the less he has. There is no escaping it.

CHAPTER 25

Keeping the Cabinet Locked Up

IN FORMER SECRETARY of Labor Robert Reich's plaintive memoir, *Locked Inside the Cabinet,* he accurately summons the extent to which the Clinton White House, and most administrations, work to keep their cabinet members under control.

While cabinet secretaries usually take office filled with an almost naive enthusiasm about the administration they are entering, they soon fall under the sway of the enormous and well-established bureaucracies they administer.

Like mini-presidents, each cabinet officer is a lord over his own manor. Served by thousands of workers anxious to impress and to move up, they are constantly tempted to emerge in the public light on a stage the president himself would have liked to have occupied. Typically, cabinet secretaries enter the administration with well-established reputations in their field of specialty or with ongoing political careers. The job of a cabinet member is hybrid. Sometimes, a cabinet secretary acts with self-serving independence as a public figure in his own right. Other times, he acts with the subservience expected of a staff member. A cabinet secretary can go either way: he can work for himself or for the president.

The key to handling the cabinet is to be sure that the media events and issue agendas its staffs cook up are served to the press at the White House, not at each cabinet department. When the agriculture secretary closes down vendors who fraudulently sell liquor or drugs for food stamps, when the Immigration and Naturalization Service raids employers of illegal aliens, or when the Justice Department indicts banks for drug money laundering, the president needs to be there to take the credit.

The president needs his staff to pick clean the legislative agendas of the individual departments, their proposed regulations and their executive actions, to bring to the White House those initiatives the president needs or wants for himself. President Clinton's tobacco regulations, food safety standards, and TV ratings system, all key actions of his presidency, could easily have been announced at the agency level, squandering the political credit. Instead, he announced them himself, getting the political reward he needed and deserved.

Cabinet-level bodies like the National Economic Council and the Domestic Policy Council can take over a presidency. Their role model, the National Security Council, runs foreign policy and would like to manage economic and domestic policy as thoroughly. A president should regard both groups with suspicion.

When President Clinton began to move to the center in the middle of his first term, Robert Reich was heard to remark at an Economic Policy Council meeting that "we don't run economic policy here anymore, it's run elsewhere." The reason, he said, was that "we aren't giving the president what he wants."

In fact, the Economic Policy Council became more of a hindrance to President Clinton as he turned his attention to welfare reform, a balanced budget, tax credits for college, and a capital-gains tax cut. Marching to the beat of its own drummer, the Council began to forget who was president and demanded that Clinton listen to its liberal opinions.

When frustrated, cabinet secretaries and their staffs often leak to the press to get their own way. A cabinet member is most effective when he forgets that he has a department of paper pushers working underneath him and becomes a close personal advisor to the chief executive—in short, when he mimics the behavior of a White House staff member.

In the Clinton administration, Secretary of Housing and Urban Development Henry Cisneros became the president's most trusted advisor on urban problems by offering his thoughts quietly and privately and taking no personal umbrage if they were not adopted. Similarly, Education Secretary Richard Reilly played the key role in guiding education policy because he respected the confidentiality of his advice to the president.

On the other hand, cabinet members who spoke publicly or used leaks to advance their policies usually infuriated President Clinton. Among the chief offenders was Secretary of Health and Human Services Donna Shalala, who once leaked to the press that Clinton was considering a value-added tax to fund his healthcare reforms, information that was news to the president.

The cabinet member who is willing to set his ego aside and realize that he has more power as a presidential advisor than as a department head is usually the most effective.

CHAPTER 26

The Post-Hillary First Lady

HILLARY CLINTON HAS REDEFINED the role of first lady. It will likely never be the same again. She has permanently subordinated the ceremonial and social role that defined the job in past administrations to the new roles of advocate and policy advisor. In a sense, Hillary has functioned as an alternate vice president, representing her husband at political events, providing key advice, acting as a political supporter and lightning rod, and functioning almost as a member of the ticket.

The question is which of these roles will last: the social role, the advocacy role, or the role as a backstage advisor.

It is for her backstage activity that Hillary has drawn the most criticism. Americans are deeply and congenitally suspicious of hidden power. The voice that whispers in his ear has long been worrisome to voters—especially when it speaks at night over a pillow.

Likely, the real role that Nancy Reagan played as a virtual member of President Reagan's staff was not far distant from the power Hillary Clinton exercises at her husband's side. But because it was hidden, private, and behind closed doors, it was not a source of major public disapproval. The suspicion about the first lady's power is aggravated by the basic changes taking place in our system—a more sophisticated electorate and a greater insistence on direct democracy.

As the amount of information available about politics has increased geometrically in recent years, so has the parlor game of guessing about the first lady's influence. With talk radio and cable TV to lend a loud and repetitive voice to what would once have been discussed in discreet whispers, the impact of an activist first lady arousing public suspicions is greater than it has ever been.

As Americans fell more pasionate about views and are unwilling to delegate decisions to others, hidden influences on a president will bring about an almost visceral jealousy in voters.

Is the first lady to be cowed into silence as a result of voter worries about her power? Not at all. It is hidden power they resent, not public advocacy. Voters want the first lady to raise her voice from the platform. As much as they distrust her behind-the-scenes role, her advocacy of public issues excites them and kindles enthusiasm, not resentment.

The more the first lady is seen as powerful, the less room a president has to be strong. She can be his most trusted advisor and exercise enormous influence, but she must work overtime at cloaking it so as not to hurt her husband.

In early 1995, President Clinton's image was bedeviled by two big negatives: immorality and weakness. About a third of the voters cited each when they volunteered their criticisms of the chief executive. Those who saw Clinton as immoral proved intractable. Their anger over his abortion and gay-rights policies resonated with their dislike of his sex life and draft-dodging. Nothing could or did bring them back.

But the voters who saw Clinton as weak and vacillating were largely responding to the impression that Hillary ran the White House. Most could not imagine that a strong wife would marry and work with a strong husband in a strong marriage. Rather, they saw the power flow between them as a zero-sum game where she held sway only at his expense.

In the first two years of the Clinton presidency, this basic misconception of the dynamics of the Clinton marriage sapped the president daily of the image of strength that his strong advocacy of healthcare reform and deficit reduction, and his courage in raising taxes, should have earned him. The public was all too ready to believe that the first lady held the real power. Precisely because they fear unelected and unaccountable power so much, they are always vigilant in checking out the first couple's marriage to be sure that she is not running the country.

Barbara Bush's adroitness in seeming totally nonpolitical made her an adorable, unthreatening figure to most Americans. At the end of the Bush presidency, her popularity so outstripped his that she appeared on camera advocating his reelection in several commercials. Roslaynn Carter attracted her share of negatives, but the obvious lack of direction of the Carter presidency made it hard for anyone to impute power-grabbing to either of them.

But Hillary so obviously relished her role in the White House that she made herself into a target for Clinton's critics. Throughout Bill's career, Hillary has frequently served as a lightning rod, deliberately attracting the fire that would otherwise be aimed at her husband. During the 1992 Republican National Convention, she was castigated by speaker after speaker. The GOP seemed to have forgotten which Clinton was appearing on the ballot. Leaving Bill Clinton largely unscathed, the 1992 Republican convention was one of the only ones in American history not to produce any gain in the polls for its candidate. (The average gain per convention over the postwar period has been a ten-point bounce).

As painful as the attacks on Hillary were to the president, the brickbats aimed at her during the first term—and as of this writing, in the second term as well—have done little to dent his popularity. But they did take their toll on her. Throughout the 1996 campaign, Clinton's favorability rating hovered around 60–35 while Hillary's ranged around 50–45.

Oddly, it was the power Hillary had in the White House, not the scandals that came to be attached to her, that lowered her popularity. Voters did not mind her supposed roles in the Rose law firm, travel office, Whitewater, and FBI file scandals nearly as much as they did her behind-the-scenes work in helping run the administration.

For all the negatives Hillary attracted by her hidden power, her public advocacy of issues affecting women and children earned her tremendous popularity. Americans want their first lady not to be silent, but to speak out in public—not in private. They want her to be an advocate of causes, not an author of legislation. They need to see her fighting for her beliefs on the platform, not for her favored nominees or political agendas in private meetings. When the news magazines begin to cover the first lady as a power center, the president is in trouble. But when she speaks in public, it is usually a big help.

Many politicians rely heavily on the political advice of their wives, but they do so in private and that makes all the difference. A president needs to realize that the public is prepared to impute incredible power to his wife. The press is waiting to write the story of her hidden influence. Only the most deliberate attempts to douse the story can even begin to keep it under control. The two keys to managing this public sensitivity are to see that the first lady has a visible, substantive, public advocacy role and to be careful dealing with the White House staff.

The only way to sell the idea that the first lady is *not* running the country is to promote what she is doing. The more she speaks out on issues of concern to her, the less the public will speculate on what else she is doing behind the scenes. It is a vacuum, not public advocacy, that stimulates their suspicion of her power.

Presidential staff members are especially sensitive to the hidden power of the first lady. It seems like dirty pool to them that their policy recommendations, so forcefully argued in Oval Office meetings, can be undone so easily in the residence. Whenever they see the first lady exercising power, they are quick to leak to the press. Thus begins a cycle especially deadly to the president.

Whatever role the first lady has in influencing a president's decisions must be kept from the staff. Recognizing that her negatives were hurting her husband, Hillary Clinton followed a careful policy of never attending a staff strategy meeting about the campaign until she began to participate in pre-convention planning after two years of voluntarily absenting herself from the process of campaign direction. She was careful never to show her hand to the White House staff.

Hillary obviously plays a role as "defender in chief" in her husband's administration, which will probably be unique in history. Unless we assume that the congruence of a sexually active president, a loyal first lady, and a prurient special prosecutor is likely to repeat itself, there is not much likelihood of this role becoming a staple part of the job.

The more permanent contribution of Hillary to the institutional history of the first lady's role will be the substantive expansion into the realm of policy advocacy.

Except for Eleanor Roosevelt, all other first ladies have confined their advocacy to safe causes—drugs, illiteracy, hunger, et cetera. It will be Hillary's lasting contribution that she manned the frontier of policy advocacy with her advanced views of the need for a federal role in education and child-rearing.

One can imagine that few future first ladies will want to endanger themselves by assuming as high a political profile in their husband's administration as she has. But hopefully, her public advocacy will set a precedent for the future.

CHAPTER 27

The Vice President

T HE VICE PRESIDENT is to the president as the queen is to the chess player: the single most valuable piece. He is potentially the most important member of the administration. Yet, only the Carter-Mondale and the Clinton-Gore relationships seem to have risen to this level. In depriving themselves of such a relationship with their VPs, other American presidents have made major mistakes.

The intimate relationship between President Clinton and Vice President Gore should probably be the role model for future administrations. But it is unlikely that we will often see the combination of a president who is not at all territorial and a vice president who rigidly follows the president's priorities at all times and in all circumstances.

One of President Clinton's most endearing traits is his almost total absence of ego. Pride, jealousy, envy are almost totally missing in his personality. It is easy for him to cede power to a vice president because he is so unpossessive of it himself.

But the generic lesson of the Clinton-Gore rapport is to choose a vice president out of love, not convenience. Tickets that are "balanced" cause relationships that are unbalanced, to the detriment of the administration.

Eisenhower looked for a young running mate from among the party faithful and chose Nixon. Kennedy recruited Johnson to help him carry Texas. Johnson sought to attract liberals to his cause by choosing a liberal like Humphrey. Reagan tapped Bush to unite the party. Bush sought a younger image and chose Quayle. Each man chose his vice president for the wrong reasons. None of them could use their vice president the way Carter used Mondale or Clinton uses Gore.

The political role of the vice presidential nominee has changed as the electorate's sophistication has increased. Traditionally, presidential candidates chose VPs to balance the ticket geographically or ideologically. In doing so, they chose the opposite of themselves. But Gore's role was not to balance the ticket, but to help explain it to the voters. It was not that Gore was different from Clinton, but the fact that he was like him, that helped the ticket.

Since Gore was a more familiar figure on the national landscape than was Clinton, his selection served to emphasize to the voters the kind of man Clinton was. Gore's youth, vigor, and modernity underscored Clinton's own. His Southern heritage reinforced Clinton's. Gore's presence did not balance Clinton's candidacy, it elaborated it. He augmented Clinton's appeal to environmentalists, an area where the Arkansas governor's good intentions had not always been matched by achievements.

When the Clintons and his own family campaigned together, Gore noted that "the whole is greater than the sum of its parts." Their collective image of youth and their telegenic families attracted the voters.

But it is serving as vice president that Gore has made his true mark. Clinton assigns Gore responsibility for literally dozens of areas.

In each, Gore turns in a capable, loyal job. His writ extends to the environment, global warming, the ozone layer, science, NASA, technology, defense contracts, wiring schools for computers, tobacco regulation, TV ratings, nuclear stockpiles in Russia, government efficiency, family-leave policies, and many other areas.

Gore is Clinton's ideal staff member: able, loyal, self-effacing. The weekly meetings between Clinton and Gore are held religiously and permit the freest exchanges of views. For his part, Clinton treats Gore as a stockholder in the administration. To Clinton, Gore is a co-owner. Everybody else is either an ally, an adversary, or the hired help.

Even when Clinton was down and out after the 1994 elections, Gore stayed loyal. He is constantly discreet in what he says and always backs Clinton as much as he can. For his part, Clinton honors this marriage made in heaven by actively promoting Gore's candidacy to succeed him.

A president has to work to make his vice president effective. Beyond just appointing him, he has to be sure his VP is not torn to pieces by the White House staff. The typical presidential staff resents the vice president even more than they do the first lady. They fear his power as they do hers, but they are better able to snub him without incurring the chief executive's wrath. By restricting his staff, limiting his flow of information, and spreading word that the VP is powerless, they constantly undermine his power.

Almost every VP has had his problem with the president's staff. In the first years of the Clinton presidency, the staff treated Gore as an outsider. Gore was particularly conscious that trusted Clinton aide George Stephanopolous had formerly been on the staff of House Speaker Dick Gephardt, then a possible rival for the 2000 Democratic nomination.

In the Bush White House, there was tension between the president's staff and Vice President Quayle. President Reagan's staff usually treated Bush as an outsider. Gerald Ford's staff saw Nelson Rockefeller as an albatross they were anxious to shed, and Nixon's people regarded Spiro Agnew as impeachment insurance—as long as Spiro was next in line, Nixon was safe.

The dislike between the staff and the vice president is rather like that between in-laws. Their relationship is the consequence of the president's marriage to the vice president. It is not a choice of their making, yet they have to live with it. The resentment, jealousy, and spite that come to the surface are legendary.

Only if the president deliberately cedes power to the vice president and forces his staff to serve both of their needs can a vice president be effective. The key to having an effective vice president is to make the staff see him as their master.

The best way to empower a vice president is to cede substantive areas to his control. Even though President Kennedy's disenfranchisement of Vice President Lyndon Johnson is widely recognized, he set a most important precedent in assigning space exploration and NASA to his vice president. President Clinton has followed this course in assigning a huge portion of the administration's agenda to Gore's care.

There is no blessing in politics more important than a skilled, top-level politician who is dedicated, loyal, and competent. It's well worth a vice presidency in return. Future presidents would be foolish to choose as their running mates anyone who they would not consider their top choice for chief of staff—or their second choice for president.

CHAPTER 28

Father Knows Best

AMERICANS HAVE ALWAYS wanted the president to be a fatherly figure. Those who have fully invested the image—FDR, Eisenhower, and Reagan—have been the most beloved. Presidents who never quite rose to the paternal level—Carter, Ford, Nixon, Johnson, and Truman—have been markedly less popular. Only John Kennedy, coming after the passivity and benign indulgence of Eisenhower, was able to lead the nation as a peer.

But because of Kennedy's unique example, political leaders have never quite understood the importance of being a father figure. John Kennedy's obvious youth, vigor, and charisma, coupled with his bold inaugural assertion that the "torch has been passed to a new generation of Americans," led to a sense that people want youth in the White House. But even if there is another politician with Kennedy's charm and attractiveness, it is unlikely that we will see a press sufficiently willing to leave the image untouched.

Ronald Reagan's paternal friendliness epitomized the style, which resonated deeply with the American people. Reliability, trustworthiness, steadiness, and unflappability became attributes Americans wanted in a president. Even in the Democratic primaries of 1984, Walter Mondale defeated Gary Hart by using an ad featuring a ringing red telephone, presumably the hot line with Moscow. The announcer asked if the voters wouldn't prefer an experienced hand like Mondale's to answer the ringing summons rather than the young, untried Gary Hart.

With Clinton, the World War II generation relinquished its thirty-two-year control of the White House. Skipping entirely the generation born between the mid-1920s and early 1940s, the baby boomers took the presidency.

In his Arkansas years, Clinton ran for governor as the electorate's son. Editorial cartoonists drew the boy governor in a baby carriage. When he succeeded in regaining office after his 1980 defeat, the carriage acquired the treads and turret of a tank, but a carriage it remained. As a candidate for president, Clinton campaigned as Everyman's friend. Happy to dine at McDonald's and Burger King, jogging in tattered shorts, fighting to control his waistline, Bill Clinton was Bubba, the regular guy running for office.

But Clinton the regular guy came across as a bumbler in the opening years of his presidency. His inability to appoint an attorney general who could be confirmed by the Senate, his gaffe in opening his administration by urging that gays be allowed in the military, and his stumbling over the economic-stimulus package left him with a look of inexperience and incompetence. The need for a greater dignity and stature became obvious. But could a young man be the nation's father? Even as his hair whitened, his suits darkened, and his ties reddened, it was unclear he could pull it off.

It is one of his most interesting achievements that even as his perpetual adolescence became glaringly obvious with each scorned woman, Clinton was able to become America's father. He did it by conscious manipulation. He featured issues involving children and was so often seen with adoring youngsters that the father image began to sink in. His platforms were always dignified; he moved his jogging indoors. He stopped his self-conscious explanations of past failures and frank confessions, which used to dot his speeches. Fathers don't explain. They don't apologize. They don't show vulnerability. Only when forced to the wall by the Lewinsky scandal did he permit a breach in his wall of dignity.

Dignity, often called presidentiality, is an essential element of a successful presidency. Jimmy Carter earned himself no credit by walking in his own inaugural parade. America, lacking a reigning monarch, looks to Hollywood for glitz and to the White House for grandeur.

A president must seem to be above it all. When he gets involved in the nitty-gritty of lobbying or seems to be his own congressional floor leader, he becomes a prime minister and loses his grip on the presidency. He must always be unrattled, calm, possessed, and sure of himself.

Ceremonial occasions are crucial for an effective chief executive. These rituals of democracy serve to elevate the president and put him above politics. The problem is to get the media to cover the events, since they are predictable, repetitive, and scripted. By combining policy with pomp, the presidential event, ceremonial or not, can make it into the nightly news.

In 1996, while greeting the largely female American winners of medals in the Atlanta Olympics, President Clinton spoke out about the need for gender equality in funding programs for female athletes in public schools. While receiving the winners of the Boys' Club public-service awards, he called for mandatory community-service requirements for high school graduation. The ceremonial and the political had been merged so the ceremonial would get covered.

At the start of his presidency, Clinton would often speak of rites he had to perform "because I'm president," as if the stature of the position were rented, like a tuxedo for a friend's wedding. After the dignity of the office became second nature to him, he internalized it and developed a presence that increasingly looked presidential.

The obvious partisanship of the Republicans in Congress enhanced Clinton's stature by comparison. The more Congress wallowed in scandal investigations and political attacks, the more Clinton appeared larger, more positive, and less political. In a classic example of jujitsu, the fury of the GOP attack made the country yearn for a president who could cast a disdaining, confident, fatherly glance at the furor in Congress. As politics sank to an all-time low of sleaze, Clinton seemed to rise in stature, even though he was, in large part, responsible for the sleaze. It was not until his direct involvement in the Lewinsky affair undermined his image of dignity that his personal popularity began to fade, even though his job approval rating remained strong.

In our democratic society, where familiarity and folksiness is at a premium, few politicians truly grasp the importance of the father image. Ronald Reagan mastered the role of president-as-father long before he entered the office. Like an experienced actor playing a role, dignity came easily to him. George Bush's success in exuding fatherliness, particularly during the Gulf War, likely came from his study at the master's knee while he served as vice president. Jimmy Carter never tried to be the nation's father. Richard Nixon couldn't pull it off. And Lyndon Johnson just looked phony.

But a president needs to play the part until he *becomes* it. He must act with the dignity his office demands long before he really feels like a president. Dignity is a political weapon every president needs.

CHAPTER 29

The Domestic Uses of Foreign Policy

MOST CONVENTIONAL THINKERS say that foreign policy doesn't matter in American domestic elections. Unless there is a war or a threat from abroad, the pundits maintain that Americans don't care about what happens past the ocean's edge. But this wisdom ignores the key role foreign policy plays in telling us about the personality of our leaders. It is on the foreign stage that we see most clearly the strengths and shortcomings of our presidents and other elected high officials.

Obviously, the use of force in foreign affairs can erase an image of weakness and vacillation, leaving an impression of resolution and toughness in its place. President George Bush, for example, never heard himself described as a wimp once he had bested Saddam Hussein in the Gulf War of 1991. President Kennedy came to be seen as callow and inexperienced after he botched the Bay of Pigs attack and the Vienna summit meeting with Khrushchev in the inauspicious first year of his tenure. But when JFK faced down the Soviets in the 1962 Cuban missile crisis, he entered history as a firm leader who wouldn't flinch in the face of danger.

But toughness is only one possible quality of leadership that foreign-policy actions can demonstrate. President Clinton has been particularly successful in establishing a reputation for patience, empathy, reliability, resourcefulness, idealism, and subtle diplomacy in his repeated and usually successful interventions in global trouble spots. His ability to bring the warring parties together in Northern Ireland and in the occupied West Bank showed Americans how their president's ability to charm and cajole could help preserve world peace.

Indeed, the very defects which characterize Clinton's image are transformed, as if through alchemy, into assets when played out on a foreign stage. His ideological flexibility, desire to please everybody, and constant wish to have it both ways madden his domestic critics, but these shortcomings have become the crucial tools of his foreign policy. Able to make everyone feel he knows their pain, empathizes with their position, and secretly wants to do all he can to help them, President Clinton has been able to win the trust of such obvious antagonists as Israeli Premier Benjamin Netanyahu and Palestinian leader Yasser Arafat.

Similarly, President Jimmy Carter's preoccupation with detail may have led to an unduly myopic presidency, but it was this very capacity to discuss patiently each square kilometer of sand in the Sinai which made the Camp David accords between Egypt and Israel possible. A Ronald Reagan might have found the minutiae maddening and remained aloof, but Jimmy Carter seemed to seek it out and used each deal over each detail to build a basis of trust between Anwar Sadat and Menachem Begin.

But if foreign policy is misplayed, it can hurt an incumbent's image faster than can domestic errors. Pocketbook issues may mean more to voters, but foreign wars, replete with atrocities, suffering, starvation, rape, and violence make much better television. The appalling images that emerge from places like Bosnia, Lebanon, Rwanda, and

Somalia can rapidly galvanize public sentiment for decisive action. A president who ignores popular emotion does so at his own peril.

Failing to act in the face of such vivid scenes of disaster quickly gives a president a reputation for weakness, ineffectuality, and dithering. As graphic pictures of suffering in Bosnia filled TV screens, President Clinton complained in 1995 that "the TV reporters are doing their damnedest to get me to enter a war."

But support for foreign intervention is paper-thin in the United States. Polling indicates that about 35 percent of the elec-torate—about twenty points from the right and fifteen points from the left—want no foreign involvement. Isolationism was never defeated at the polls. For the left, it was discredited when Hitler attacked Russia, and for the right, it fell when our battleships sank at Pearl Harbor. But it remains a potent force in both political parties.

With only about two-thirds of voters willing to tolerate any foreign action at all, for any reason, a president doesn't have much margin for error before he loses his political support in the face of foreign reversals.

The best way to sell foreign involvement to Americans is not through appeals to nationalism or economic self-interest but to look instead at human rights and values to generate support. The career officials of the State Department and the National Security Council don't get it. They believe in the maxim that war is "diplomacy by other means." To them, issues like the stability of the Western alliance or the need for global harmony are paramount concerns. They are willing to stoop to citing economic interests like trade or jobs to sell their policies. But they regard appeals to human values as mushy, unreliable, and dangerous because they might require more action than we bargained for.

But it is only through a focus on the abuse of people—par-ticularly children—that the American people are willing to rise above their essentially isolationist prejudices. They could care less about diplomacy or alliances, and appeals to economic self-interest ring hollow in times of economic boom.

For all the focus on questions of character and scandal that have become chapter and verse of our politics these days, it is not in the bedroom but in the situation room that Americans learn the most about the personalities and character of their leaders. The tests of foreign policy—of toughness, compassion, courage, and resourcefulness—are the real ways that character count in evaluating a president.

For the Truman presidency, the defining moments that told us what kind of man we had as president were the Truman Doctrine to save Greece and Turkey, the Marshall Plan to save Europe, and the decision to act in the face of aggression in Korea.

For Eisenhower, it was his willingness to stay patient and restrained in the face of Khrushchev's insults during the 1960 Paris summit. For Kennedy, it was the Cuban missile crisis. For Johnson, it was his bungling of the war in Vietnam. For Nixon, it was his deftness in opening a relationship with China. For Carter, it was Camp David on the positive side and the hostage crisis in Iran on the negative. For Reagan, it was his bombing of Libya and his outreach to Gorbachev that were pluses, and the Iran-Contra scandal that was a negative. For Bush, it was the Gulf War that defined his foreign policy.

The conventional wisdom may marginalize the impact of foreign policy, but history suggests that it is in this arena more than any other that presidents are made or broken.

PART 3

Getting Elected

Obviously, our new political era changes the way candidates must run when they seek elective office. The changing levels of voter sophistication have so altered our electoral landscape that the vast bulk of what now constitutes the conventional wisdom about elections is obsolete. Starting with the first step, sizing up a race, and proceeding to the end, we must reevaluate what candidates do, how to run, and how to win.

CHAPTER 30

Should I Run?

W HEN IS IT SAFE to go into the electoral waters? When should a man or a woman run?

If running means taking on an incumbent, check out the calendar. Successful insurgencies are typically concentrated in certain years. In figuring out whether or not to take on an incumbent, it is most important to decide whether the times are ripe for change.

Some election years are partisan debacles for the left or the right. In the 1958 recession, the 1964 Goldwater disaster, the 1974 Watergate elections, and the 1986 midterm races, Republicans lost dramatically. The 1972 Nixon landslide, the 1980 Reagan housecleaning, and the 1994 anti-Clinton outpouring were equally dismal for the Democrats.

The strange thing about partisan sweeps is that we rarely see them coming far in advance. It is only in hindsight, or in the few weeks before election day, that its dimensions become apparent. Pundits will always hedge their predictions near the 50-yard line, generally seeing only moderate gains or losses. That way, they avoid being wrong at the top of their lungs. But each potential challenger needs to make his or her own independent assessment of the times. In recent history, about one election in three is marked by a radical turnover in power. The most important question for any potential candidate is, "Is this my year?"

In bad economic times or in an era ripped by scandal, insurgents find the wind at their backs. But public boredom can just as surely enhance a challenger's chances. When political cycles have run their course, the old actors must often leave the stage—voluntarily or by defeat. In the 1986 congressional elections, two years after Ronald Reagan was overwhelmingly reelected, his Republican Senate majority collapsed. The events that constituted the Iran-Contra scandal had not yet been made public. The economy was doing fine. Reagan's job approval ratings were very high. Yet, the president's men were mowed down by insurgent Democrats. The public understood that it was time to change faces. The voters realized that the Senate soldiers of the Reagan revolution had done their bit and had no more to contribute. It was time for them to go.

Whether through public anger or through boredom, voters usually have to be in the mood for change for challengers to win. Yet, weak incumbents can be defeated even in relatively stable years, and hardy ones can survive even the worst epidemics of public anger. Polls designed to measure the vulnerability of an incumbent usually miss the key point. Pollsters and their clients too often focus on the popularity or job rating of an incumbent in deciding if he can be defeated. This is a bit like seeing if a tree can be chopped down by measuring its height.

The issue is not whether the incumbent is popular but whether people really know what he or she is all about. A senator with a reputation in his home state as a moderate, but with a voting record that is really far left or far right, may be very vulnerable despite a 70 percent approval rating. On the other hand, Senator Jesse Helms (R-NC) regularly scores negatively in popularity polls but constantly wins because voters know who he is, know the good and the bad, and want him anyway.

Frequently, senators score higher in public ratings than do governors or mayors, yet are more vulnerable to defeat. By the time a president, a governor, or a mayor runs for reelection, voters know all about them. The incessant media coverage of chief executives usually shows all an incumbent's warts long before election day. This gives the office-holder time to repair the damage or to offset it with positive achievements. By election day, voters are frequently deaf to the insurgent's negatives against the incumbent because it is all old news. Thus, Reagan or Clinton will be said to be coated with Teflon—charges don't stick—because voters know so much about them that new information, positive or negative, has little impact.

On the other hand, people rarely read about the daily doings of a United States senator. When an opponent attacks the incumbent senator's record, it's likely to be news to the voter. We meet our senators only every six years when they run, while we see our executive-branch officials every day in print. The daily drubbing presidents, mayors, and governors get in the media may lower their poll numbers, but may confer a kind of immunity to attack that legislative officials do not enjoy.

Congressmen are a breed apart. They almost never lose. They are protected by the xenophobia (fear of strangers) of the American public. Daily, we face the grim knowledge that our government can destroy any of us. The danger that close scrutiny of our tax returns might pose, the possibility of an unwelcome visit from a government regulator, or our dependence on Treasury checks all brings us a sense of personal vulnerability. We try not to think about it too much but when we do, it is terrifying. We can be ruined by an overzealous tax auditor or public prosecutor, or even by careless clerk making a typographical error on our file.

Facing an alien government, we see our congressman as the friendly intermediary. His familiar face assuages our panic toward the cold institutions of government that face us. Strident campaigns against incumbent congressmen usually backfire, since they throw ice on the cozy relationship we tend to feel with our local representative. Senators are too distant to benefit from this intimacy, but congressmen, who run every two years, are very close indeed.

Congressman Mark Andrews served North Dakota throughout the 1960s and 1970s as the state's sole congressman. Elected statewide every two years, he had an intimacy with the voters of his taciturn state that made him invulnerable to serious challenge. In 1980, he was elected U.S. senator. He had moved from one statewide job to another. But he had to run every six years, instead of every two. By 1986, he seemed weakened politically, and polled to find out why. In the key question, he asked voters if he had been a better congressman or senator. He lost the race to himself. By 3-to-1 they said he had been better in his old job. As a senator they found him remote, removed, distant, and arrogant. He had lost the daily familiarity that keeps congressmen in office. He had become a stranger. Xenophobia had set in. He was defeated for reelection.

The only real way to beat a congressman is to get closer to the people than he is. Like Anna in *The King and I*, an insurgent must work to keep his head lower than the incumbent's at all times. State legislators, with smaller districts and more proximity than congressmen who must stay in Washington, often make the best challengers because they offer the same relief of xenophobia that keeps a congressman in business. Those who run ideological races for Congress generally lose. With the intimacy of the relationship between congressmen and their constituents, what's a policy disagreement between friends?

Despite Gingrich's success in nationalizing the elections of 1994 by fighting on a nationwide platform against Clinton and his healthcare plan, the American system is not a parliamentary one but is based on separation of the legislative and executive branches. It is usually only by mimicking the intimacy of a congressman that an insurgent can hope to prevail.

A good way to beat a congressman in an election is to lose the previous one. Defeat in a congressional district is a growth process in which challengers become more familiar and accepted by the xenophobic electorate. Newt Gingrich himself ran and lost several times before he finally secured election to the House of Representatives. While losing a statewide race usually destroys a candidate's ability to run again, losing a House race often is just paying the dues toward an ultimate victory.

When you look for a rent-controlled apartment in New York City, it is usually better to consult the obituary page than the classifieds. The same is true in searching for an office from which to launch a political career. Races against incumbents are risky ways to enter politics, best reserved for the chronically impatient. By contrast, open seats seem to beckon amateurs and novices. In some states, term limits imposed by voters hasten the departure of incumbents. In other places, the innate frustration level of a political career takes its toll and creates vacancies. If a political aspirant waits long enough, he's likely to find the vacant high-backed leather chair of his dreams and run for an open seat.

If the general rule on challenging incumbents is, *Don't unless you must*, the axiom concerning open seats is, *If you are at all serious about politics, give it a shot*. For the ambitious, life doesn't get any better than a vacancy in a higher office.

To win an election, a candidate must usually have high name recognition, access to money, an issue that will carry his candidacy, or an organization gorged with manpower. If you don't have any of these attributes, you've got to develop at least one of them.

You can develop name recognition through hard work and door-to-door contact in a small district. By ruthlessly expanding and exploiting one's expanded social and family circle, a candidate can generate access to funds. One can build a campaign organization by identifying with a cause or a local group of activists. Anyone can find a good issue.

But vacancies in politics occur suddenly and, usually, unexpectedly. Few people can develop new name recognition, sudden access to money, or an organization of believers in a few weeks or months. It takes awhile. It even takes time to become identified with an issue that can carry a candidacy. Voters don't trust overnight conversions.

So, the ambitious must prepare to run for a vacancy long before it eventuates. Gingrich won his House majority after years of tenacious work by GOPAC, his political-action arm, in cultivating candidates and helping them prepare for the moment of truth when they actually ran. Newt correctly understood that it takes years of preparation to lay the basis for a sudden success in electoral politics.

The secular equivalent of the spiritual injunction to "live each day as if it were your last" is each year to act as if this were the year when an office will open up. Prospective candidates must work each day to expand their base of financial support, spread their name recognition, enhance their political organizations, and heighten their identification with important issues, even when there is no vacancy in sight.

In his audacious study of American politicians, *The United States of Ambition*, Alan Ehrenfield details how candidates build the elements of support they will need for their maiden runs for elective office. The multiplicity of paths novices take to reach the day when they launch their first candidacy is dazzling.

The most common is service on the staff of a local elected official. A young man or woman who is paid to handle constituent problems or to work with local groups on community issues has a big advantage when an electoral office opens up. But the paths to politics can run through success in business, a platform in media, a military career, or a law practice with a large client base. It can even run through a North Vietnamese POW camp or a voyage to the moon.

The key element is to assess any activity from the vantage of how it will aid in name recognition, campaign funding, access to an organization, or development of an issue identification. The local dog-catcher can build his constituency if he diligently eyes these objectives as he chases Fido around the block.

In an open-seat election, a jack-of-all-trades doesn't usually make it. A candidate must have a clear edge in at least one category. A little money, some name recognition, a small organization, and a so-so issue won't get the job done. An initial candidacy must be based on mastery of at least one of these elements.

A candidate with access to money, organization, or preexisting name recognition is indeed blessed. But at higher levels of electoral politics, Congress on up, *issues* play the key role. Unless a candidate can define what his candidacy is about, he cannot project the coherence he needs to win. Anyone with an issue can attract money, recognition, and an organization. Finding the issue is the key problem.

CHAPTER 31

Choosing Your Issue

ISSUES ARE THE VOCABULARY of politics. Skeptical voters will not accept self-congratulatory descriptions of a candidate's attributes and virtues in paid advertisements. Neither will they permit themselves to draw inferences from the handsome, honest faces of candidates with rugged jaws they see paraded before them. Voters have been burned too often.

So, political candidates need to use the vocabulary of issues to tell voters who they are. Those attributes the electorate refuses to infer from images, it will willingly learn from issue positions. A strong stand against car insurance premiums will show an understanding about the problems of the average family far more credibly than will a mom-and-pop scene around the kitchen table. Support for mandatory sentences for violent crimes will show toughness much better than a muscular candidate with a grim countenance slamming a jail-cell door shut with a clang. Ultimately, it is not the issue itself that is crucial; it is what a candidate's advocacy of a specific cause says about his values and philosophy. Issues become a form of symbolic speech, an opportunity to speak to a candidate's character and attributes.

But issues have a short half-life. After a few years, their political potency is gone and they lose their effectiveness. Abortion, school busing, term limits, school prayer, the death penalty, immigration, and the like have been such staples of our polarized dialogue that they have tended to lose their impact. The voters who care deeply about these issues still see them as relevant, but most other voters dismiss them. Once an issue has been overused, its value as a form of symbolic speech ebbs. Voters begin to see advocacy of the position as a means of electoral manipulation, not as an indication of a deeply felt conviction. When a candidate advocates the death penalty, he gets points only for political acumen, not for courage or toughness.

In 1996, President Clinton's lead dwindled to single digits in the final week before the election because he overused the Medicare issue. "I know it," Clinton recalled with rueful hindsight, "we stayed with Medicare for too long. We should have talked about Head Start or nursing homes or the environment." The Medicare issue had lost its punch by election day.

Once voters read in *Time* magazine that an issue is being widely used by ambitious politicians, it loses its edge. For example, support for term limits implied good things about a candidate who supported them. The electorate saw support for these limits as an indication that a candidate was independent and shared their distrust of politicians. After a few years, however, backing of term limits lost its power to move voters and came to be seen as pandering to a popular position.

To work, an issue must be real. It needs to deal with a deep concern of the electorate's and must constitute a real solution in the minds of the voters. Symbolic nonsense such as flag-burning or recitation of the pledge of allegiance in schools won't do the trick anymore. The electorate has grown up.

An issue must be controversial to form the basis for selection of a candidate. Support for literacy or more research on a cure for cancer are too ecumenical to be salient. Voters need to perceive that an issue position requires courage and must know that it makes certain people mad at the candidate if they are to find the position sufficiently compelling to attract their votes. Support for motherhood and apple pie may meet with broad approval; however, none but the most gullible voter can possibly believe these positions say anything about the candidate who adopts them except to testify to his banality.

No issue is too subtle, too complex, too specific, or too abstruse for the American voter. The C-SPAN, CNN, Fox News Channel, CNBC, MSNBC, and CFN cable-TV channels, TV news shows like *60 Minutes*, *20/20*, and *Prime Time Live*, all-news radio, news talk stations, weekly national news magazines, and a host of opinion journals constantly bombard us with information. Our voters are well enough informed to tolerate surprising complexity in the public dialogue.

At the start of the 1995–1996 budget debate, many in the Clinton White House despaired of explaining the difference between the president's program of $124 billion in Medicare "savings" and Gingrich's $270 billion in "cuts." "As soon as we put out our balanced-budget alternative," George Stephanopoulos warned at the time, "Gingrich will turn right around and say, 'See, you want to cut Medicare, too.'"

But despite these misapprehensions, Clinton did succeed in explaining that he wanted to save money for Medicare by cutting doctor's fees and hospital charges while the Republicans wanted to charge the elderly more in premiums. This distinction was not lost on the voters; rather, it became an axis on which the election swung.

There is literally no such thing as an idea that cannot be expressed well and articulately to today's voters in thirty seconds. Increasing educational and informational levels make it increasingly possible to share even relatively subtle or complex thoughts in a minimum of time. Those who find this task impossible should blame themselves, not the electorate. A prominent political consultant once said that he could think "of a lot of things you could say in thirty seconds: 'I love you.' 'I'm going to kill you.' 'Will you marry me?'" The problem, he said, was that "politicians don't really have anything to say."

Just as the era of big government is dead, for now, the era of the big issue is over as well. Any big new idea is sure to be picked apart by the special interests. Like the battleships of old, omnibus programs present too tempting a target, too easily destroyed by a single attack, to make it through a fight. Flat-tax schemes, Hillary's health-care colossus, the total overhaul of environmental rule-making and regulation envisioned in the Contract With America are all dragons of the past. At the moment, voters do not feel sufficiently disillusioned with the status quo to embrace a complete, one-stop alternative. It is through incremental change after change, step after step, that a states-man of today can vindicate a bold vision.

Polling is the key to selecting the right issue. You must ask the voters a specific question and measure the intensity of their reaction to gauge the impact of an issue. Then, you need to follow up the question with arguments, first on one side, then on the other, to test its ability to survive debate. Finally, you've got to put the issue in the context of your own political situation to evaluate its strength and salience.

To test an issue's impact, a pollster needs to put each pro-posal through such a gauntlet. An issue must:

- tap into a basic concern
- meet with strong support but also attract a measure of strong opposition
- command a large majority that grows, or at least doesn't shrink, after pro and con argumentation
- significantly affect voter decisions about the election at hand.

Politicians must learn the difference between "concerns" and "issues" in choosing a positive, substantive campaign theme. A candidate has to do more than articulate a concern to distinguish his platform. He needs to focus on a specific issue to meet the concern. When voters speak of their worries about "education," politicians must speak of issues like school choice or national education standards to distinguish their candidacies. When voters talk about their concern with "crime," a politician must answer with a program—a specific issue—like gun control.

Once you have found your issue, never let it go. Insist on injecting it, through ads and news coverage, into the voters' minds again and again. Elections often become contests of alternate issues, each as well researched and prepared as the other. The winner will be the candidate who has chosen the best issue and is most persistent in sticking to it and explaining it articulately.

As noted earlier, for the moment populism seems to have run its course in American politics. Generally, populist issues focus either on economic or social discontent. Economic populism is limited because of the basic optimism of Americans who usually devoutly believe in their personal upward mobility. Social populism generally finds a truncated base because of the lack of pervasive racism or religious prejudice in America. While there are many angry white men, there are more who watch Bill Cosby on TV, root for Michael Jordan, and want to vote for Colin Powell for president. There is simply neither the reservoir of discontent to water the seeds of economic populism nor the prejudice to water those of social populism in any sustained way. Americans are usually not that angry. Indeed, only the Nixon/silent majority elections of 1968 and 1972 and the Reagan anti-government victory of 1980 were motivated by social populism. Economic populism can be said to have played a role in the 1948 Truman win and the 1992 Clinton election. But the presidential races of 1952, 1956, 1960, 1964, 1976, 1984, 1988, and 1996 were all largely devoid of the populist shadow.

The problem with populists is they think everyone agrees with them and shares their animus against the elites. But this is just not so. The social populists of the Dole campaign focused their anger on the permissive culture of the boomer generation. They ripped Clinton's draft avoidance, drug experimentation, and sexual promiscuity, but were bewildered when only white men over sixty-five fully rallied to their cause. Stunned, they kept repeating the charges louder and louder and waited for hordes of hard hats to join in their outrage. But they never showed up.

The economic populists of Clinton's left flank, James Carville, Robert Reich, and pollster Stanley Greenberg could never understand why all Americans did not share their outrage at income inequality, layoffs, and corporate downsizing. In vain they waited on the barricades, like their forebears in Victor Hugo's *Les Miserables*, for the masses who never came.

Don't Get Known Too Quickly

THE NOVICE POLITICIAN always asks, "How can I get known?" But that's the wrong question. In today's saturated media environment, getting name recognition is not the big problem. The real challenge is to become known *and* popular at the same time. As my Democratic consultant friend Hank Sheinkopf points out, "Hitler has good name recognition."

For the unknown politician, the process of getting known is full of peril and potential. Politicians who focus on name recognition without taking care to tell people their attributes and ideas at the same time often doom their own careers.

After Democratic presidential challenger Senator Gary Hart upended front-runner Walter Mondale in the New Hampshire primary of 1984, he was instantly famous. The covers of all the news magazines and the nightly TV news shows heralded his sudden rise to prominence. But Mondale strategists Bob Bekel and Roy Spence correctly sensed that Hart was now vulnerable. Voters learned that a man named Hart was advocating "new ideas" but knew nothing else. Bekel and Spence filled the gap by quoting a hamburger commercial, asking of the senator's new ideas, "Where's the beef?" Spence produced a television ad that showed a red phone on the president's desk and asked who voters trusted to make decisions of war or peace: Hart, whom they barely knew, or Mondale, who had four years under his belt as vice president of the United States? Had Hart become known more gradually and taken more care to build a simultaneous identification with concrete proposals, he could have survived this attack.

Learning from Hart's mistakes, Clinton became nationally known over a period of several months, even before New Hampshire's primary. He took care that voters learned of his positions, such as his pledge to "end welfare as we know it" and his boast that he was a "new Democrat," at the same time they learned his name. When attacks hit—over sex and the draft—voters already had positive information about the Arkansas governor to counteract the negatives they heard. Unlike Hart, Clinton survived his wounds.

Billboards, bumper stickers, buttons, or any campaign advertisement that spreads a candidate's name without also giving his message are dangerous. Name recognition opens a file in the voter's mental hard drive. A politician must take care to fill it quickly with specific positives. He may even have to slow the spread of his name recognition so that his *substantive* recognition can keep pace.

It is not enough for a candidate to stress his compassion or integrity as he acquires name recognition. These generalities will not provide sufficient immunity once the negatives start to rain down. Only concrete achievements or positions will do. Specificity is key.

When an opponent runs a negative ad attacking the candidate for raising taxes, voters will not remember the warm, feel-good positive advertisement that a candidate ran to introduce himself a few weeks before. Such an ad will provide no inoculation against the tax charge. But if a candidate has established a firm issue identification, such as opposing utility-rate increases, voters will remember his position when they hear a negative ad attacking him. "Too bad he voted for higher taxes," they might say after seeing both positive and negative ads, "but at least he's good on utility rates."

CHAPTER 33

How to Be Noticed in a Crowded Room

WHEN AN ELECTED OFFICE is vacant, the line of candidates is usually as long as those at Disney's Magic Kingdom in Orlando. Like debutantes at a ball, candidates try to single themselves out by attracting special attention.

In recent presidential races, each candidate has tried to advance his "unique selling proposition." In the 1996 Republican presidential field, for example, Dole sold himself as the man of character, Phil Gramm as the true conservative, Pat Buchanan as the truer conservative, Lamar Alexander as the outsider.

Each chose his theme to position himself against his opponents. Dole ran on character to stress Clinton's scandals; Gramm and Buchanan wanted to contrast their doctrinaire conservatism with Dole's inconsistent ideological record; Alexander sought to play off Dole's and Gramm's roles as Washington insiders. But Steve Forbes eschewed negative comparisons and used a positive idea, the flat tax, to distinguish himself. He finished strong in the early Iowa and New Hampshire primaries because voters appreciated his proposal.

Forbes' message succeeded because it was easier to believe than the messages of his opponents. If Steve Forbes says he is for a flat tax, there is no reason to doubt him. But if Dole claims to be of high moral character, and Alexander says he's an outsider, and Gramm and Buchanan claim they are ideologically consistent, how are we to know if they are telling the truth? By leading with adjectives or attributes, rather than introducing themselves over an issue as Forbes did, these candidates handicapped themselves at the start of the race.

Forbes' message also did well because it did not require that a voter dislike anyone else in order to be moved by it. To appreciate Dole's message about character, voters had to dislike Clinton. Only if voters were turned off by Dole's constant political repositioning would the Gramm or Buchanan attacks work. But there was no pre-requisite price of admission for a voter to accept Forbes' message.

Forbes ultimately failed because he chose the wrong issue—a big idea like flat taxes. Its limited popularity doomed his campaign. But by positioning himself on an issue and introducing himself to the voters through an issue, not through an adjective or an attribute, he had the right idea.

Some candidates figure that if they spend enough money, they can get the voters to believe good things about them. But it rarely works out that way. Unless an ad carries a message that is directly relevant to the lives of each voter, few will pay it much heed no matter how many times it airs. But a message that carries the right issue, one that appeals to the personal needs and concerns of a voter, is always wanted, always welcome. A candidate with a good issue can dominate a crowded race even if he is outspent by 3-to-1 or 4-to-1.

New proposals quickly grab attention and find deep resonance in the electorate. Candidate Clinton's stress on the need to prepare to compete in the global economy and the importance of welfare reform served him well. So did Eugene McCarthy's opposition to the war in Vietnam, Reagan's support for tax cuts, and Carter's pledge to restore integrity to government. These affirmative issue positions carried their candidates far and successfully distinguished them from the pack of candidates early in the race.

In a crowded field, a candidate must search for issues that radiate intensity rather than just breadth of support. An issue must have enough resonance with voters to induce them to single it out above all others as most relevant to their lives.

When a candidate faces opposition from single-issue constituencies, he can often gain the upper hand by using new ideas to counter those that are ideologically entrenched, but so frequently repeated that they have lost their punch. New ideas can defeat old, established positions if they are good enough. A candidate with a good issue can even lure away those who back his strident, single-issue opponent.

Jimmy Carter's call to restore integrity to government and "give America a government as good as its people," won over George Wallace's base in 1976. George Bush's call to continue the Reagan agenda pulled away enough of Pat Robertson's Christian base in 1988 to win the nomination. Bill Clinton's proposals on welfare reform and education drew support away from the populist reform appeal of Jerry Brown.

You just have to find the right issue.

CHAPTER 34

Managing the Dialogue

ELECTIONS ARE DEBATES between candidates over issues. The ebb and flow of the argumentation, more than the amount of money each side spends, more often than not determines who the winner will be. Managing the dialogue of a political campaign is the most important task there is. In today's politics, paid television advertising is, by far, the most effective way to win the issue debate at the core of a political race.

Pounding Your Issue Home

Once you've chosen the issue on which to base your campaign, never let it go. Push it to the forefront of the race by making it the centerpiece of your paid television advertising.

Don't begin your campaign with a biographic ad introducing yourself to the voters. They don't care. There is plenty of time to tell them who you are. Begin with issue advocacy, which compels voters to pay attention because it is their problem (high taxes), not your problem (low name recognition) that you are addressing. Voters are not especially interested in who is going to run for what next year. But they care passionately about how to solve their most pressing problems, so they'll listen to issue ads when they won't listen to biographic commercials.

Today's sophisticated electorate sets high standards for what will move them in a political commercial. A good ad should function on two levels: the rational and the emotional. The spot must identify a key problem and articulate a practical, workable proposal to fix it. Each ad must overcome public skepticism and tap into the deep reservoir of hope that animates our people. To be effective, advertisements cannot cut corners on the facts. They must be factual and realistic in order to work. Pollsters need to test the arguments in the ad and see how they stand up to rebuttals and counterattacks. Does the argument move voters and do they *stay* moved once the other side has spoken?

But even as the ad creates a factual basis for acceptance, it must also pack an emotional message. Good visuals are very effective if they enlist the emotions of the voters. Republican media expert Bob Goodman said, "I only know about four things when I create an ad—love, hope, hate, and fear." Hank Sheinkopf, a Democratic media creator, addressed these emotions in the Clinton campaign when he framed an advertisement backing a ban on assault rifles around the true story of a police officer who watched his partner die in a hail of assault-weapon fire.

Sometimes, the visual should tell a story. In Clinton's welfare-reform ad, consultants Bill Knapp and Marius Penczner teamed with Sheinkopf to tell a pictorial story of a little girl peering out her front window, waiting for her father to come home. When he appears in the driveway, lunch bucket in hand, his daughter runs to greet him on his triumphal return. The advertisement tells the message—work over welfare—in its soundtrack and, on a parallel course, in its visual. The emotional impact of this juxtaposition was extraordinary.

The key is to keep the viewer intellectually and emotionally occupied. The competition for his attention is steep: the ham sandwich and beer in the refrigerator in the next room. Media consultant Stuart Stevens says the "visual literacy" of the voters, their ability to absorb the meaning of picture messages in a few seconds, has increased dramatically. "Remember the way the old movies used to show a guy leaving his house, getting in a cab, paying the fare at the airport, boarding the plane, relaxing in his seat, descending the stairs at a foreign airport, getting in a cab, and getting out at his hotel?" Stevens says. "Now they just show the scene in one city and then the scene in the next one. People get it that he traveled." The corollary of Stevens' insight is that media that tells voters what they have already figured out on their own is redundant and boring. Advantage: ham sandwich.

In fact, ads should be a bit obscure and tense, keeping the viewer riveted while the scene unfolds. In one ad for Tennessee gubernatorial candidate Don Sundquist, also prepared by Penczner, the candidate proposed drug-testing parolees. "If they're using drugs, lock them back up," Sundquist says in the ad. "Because if they're using drugs, a robbery is sure to follow." While Sundquist spoke, Penczner's visual told its own compelling story. A gaunt, pale actor with a day's growth of beard, dressed in an undershirt and filmed in black-and-white, walked down the street holding a neatly folded brown paper bag. The suggestion that he had just been released from prison and was carrying his clothing was obvious. A van pulls alongside and an arm reaches out to beckon. It seems to say, "Come here, I've got some drugs for you." As the parolee glances nervously at the van and hesitates in his gait, a police car cruises by behind him. The former inmate thinks again and walks on. In his vacillation, we see the dilemma, the temptation, and the dangers, but also the positive possibilities in parole. Drug-testing was the obvious answer. The visual requires concentration. The ham sandwich has to wait.

The gimmicks media creators use include handheld cameras; their shaky images seem to generate a tension that holds the viewer. The faint suggestion lingers that the camera is catching the scene as it takes place, unguarded and real. Partial shots of the candidate's body: his hands, his wedding ring, his shoulder, part of his face, all create a tension within the viewer, who wants to see who it is that is being filmed. Like the chiaroscuro in the paintings of the masters, the mystery compels attention.

But visual techniques come and go. No sooner do creative media people invent one video stunt than viewers spot the manipulation and begin to guard against it. Their antibodies begin to form shortly after the ad starts to run. In a year or two, the technique has lost its appeal. The roaches have developed an immunity to this year's roach spray.

For too many media creators, the visual and the form are everything. They could care less about the actual proposal the candidate is making. More into style than substance, they constantly squeeze the message into fewer and fewer words, cutting back the arguments it needs to work. In the 1984 presidential race, when Gary Hart was under fire for a lack of specificity in his issue proposals, his media creator admitted that he found it difficult to answer Mondale's taunt—"Where's the beef?" It turned out the media man had never read Gary Hart's book, which was full of beef. He was so little concerned with Hart's substantive ideas that he never had taken the time to read the book. The image was everything.

Every candidate must remember in developing his positive ads that he or she faces a dual threat. From outside, he must make a case that satisfies the press and is so rooted in accuracy that his opponent has no rebuttal. But from within his own campaign, he must face the equal danger that his message will be lost in the creative zeal of his consultants.

Striking First

All campaigns end on election day. But they can start whenever you like. Start early. Very early. Today, for example, would be a good time.

Most elections are decided long before election day. In seven of the thirteen post-World War II presidential races, the contest was over before Labor Day (1952, 1956, 1964, 1972, 1984, 1988, and 1996). In four of the remaining races, the contests were close only because one side started out very far ahead and either blew, or almost blew, the lead (1948, 1968, 1976, and 1992). Only in 1960 and 1980 did the election's outcome seesaw until the very end, in one case to a photo finish, and in the other it suddenly tipped to Ronald Reagan, the challenger. Down-to-the-wire finishes are a lot more likely in horse-racing than in politics.

So, the advice "Don't fire until you see the whites of their eyes," is wrong.

In Clinton's come-from-behind win in 1996, he started his campaign's TV advertising eighteen months before election day. By February of 1996, ten months before the polls opened, Clinton had locked in the big lead he held throughout.

The only thing in politics one can't replace is lost time. Begin early. Set up your theme at the outset. Force voters to cope with *your* themes, *your* issues, *your* proposals, before the other side can inject theirs.

In a race against a reasonably popular incumbent, don't open with negatives attacking him. Negative ads tell the voter that your candidate, the challenger, is only right for you if you don't like the incumbent. They say that if you *do* like the incumbent, you can't vote for our man. Most victorious challengers need a great many votes from people who still like the incumbent but just like the new candidate more. Positive ads win such voters. Negative ads drive them away.

Some candidates want to hoard their money until the end and resist early spending. They don't understand the essential equation of modern political finance: $\% = \$$. Good poll numbers (%) equal more campaign contributions ($). Early media, which endows your candidacy with an aura of likely success, stimulates campaign contributions. Most donors are opportunists and all donors like to win.

Sometimes, insurgents can ambush incumbents, doing little until right before election day and then springing a surprise offensive. In 1990, candidate Paul Wellstone successfully used these tactics to defeat Republican incumbent Senator Rudy Boschwitz in Minnesota. But such efforts usually require a silver bullet that can take out an opponent with one shot. Silver bullets are rare. So start early.

Disarm Your Opponent by Agreeing with Him

It is not a God-given requirement that every candidate must disagree with every position his opponent takes or demean all of his adversary's achievements. Agreement and praise are two of the most devastating weapons in any politician's arsenal. Only when an issue is joined by an opposing point of view does it become fodder for a campaign. When both sides agree, the issue becomes a sideshow, no matter how seminal it may be to the belief structure of one of the two opposing camps.

It is each candidate's right to articulate that with which he disagrees in the program, policies, or achievements of his opponent. If he chooses to criticize any aspect of his opponent's record, then it becomes legitimate ground for debate. But if a candidate sidesteps the issue or praises and agrees with his adversary on it, the issue loses its impact on the election.

Where an opponent has a clear area of superiority, it is best to bypass it by "hugging" your adversary on that particular issue so there is no distance between your position and his.

When Ruth Messinger ran against New York's Mayor Rudy Guiliani, she faced an incumbent who had had great success in reducing dramatically the city's crime rate. She should have avoided the crime issue entirely and pounded away at Giuliani's shortcomings: education and job creation. If she had praised the mayor's crime record and said she'd keep his police commissioner on the job, the entire race would have been fought on the grounds of her critique— jobs and schools—not on Giuliani's strength. Instead, Messinger was tempted by the blatant police brutality in a Brooklyn precinct house right before the election, and criticized the mayor's police and crime policies. That statement may have gained her a few days of good press. But it let the crime issue into the election and permitted Giuliani to win in a walk.

Similarly, in 1996, Clinton agreed with Gingrich and Dole on making welfare recipients work, time limits for welfare, balancing the budget, cutting taxes, reforming government regulation, cutting the size of the federal payroll, and the death penalty. By "hugging" them on these key points, he forced the focus of the election to shift to the areas over which they disagreed: Medicare and Medicaid cuts, education and environmental programs, family-leave laws, gun control, abortion, and so forth.

The battle for control of an election is a battle of the issues against one another for saliency. Each side has issues the public cares about on which it will likely do the better job. The key is to make your strength more relevant to the voters than that of your opponent.

For example, Reagan defeated Carter in 1980 because diplomatic and military toughness in the face of the hostage crisis was the key issue. Had compassion been more central, Carter would have won. In the same vein, Bush defeated Dukakis in 1988 because crime was the most important difference. Had helping the poor been the fulcrum, Dukakis would have been elected.

The job of each candidate is to maximize his issue's chance to dominate the dialogue by presenting it in the most compelling way and underscoring the extent of his disagreement with his adversary. On the other hand, his task is also to minimize the likelihood that his opponent's issue will come to the fore by narrowing his disagreements with his opponent in these areas.

It is almost impossible to defend against an opponent who insists on praising you and agreeing with you. It's hard to push away someone who wants to hug you. But if your adversary does hug you, there goes your pet issue.

Rebutting Your Opponent's Attacks

In today's politics, rebuttal is crucial. Rebuttals usually defeat attacks.

Virtually all Republican political consultants and most Democratic ones still believe the negative ad is in ascendancy. They point to the corpses of defeated Democrats in 1994 and the success of the GOP's anti-liberal, anti-labor attacks that kept the Congress in their hands in 1996 to validate their view.

But voters are acquiring an immunity to negative advertising. They have seen the worst said about the public figures they like the best and have watched media extol the virtues of men and women who are carted off to jail a few months later. Their skepticism argues silently in their minds with the assertions that come their way in news programs, political speeches, and especially in political advertising. It is not the dialogue with one's adversary that a candidate must win. It is this quiet debate between belief and skepticism inside the voter's own mind upon which hinges the outcome of an election.

This is the key rule in a political contest: He who asserts must prove. Each statement—positive or negative—a candidate or his advertising makes subjects him to the gauntlet of voter skepticism and opposition criticism. Should his assertion prove wanting or untruthful, his misstatement will do more to kill him than the underlying issue ever would have done.

A negative ad opens up the candidate who uses it to the potentially devastating damage of his opponent's rebuttal ad. A rebuttal not only wipes out the impact of the original negative attack, but it damages the credibility of the candidate who launched the attack and makes it harder for him to attack again. A candidate who runs a negative ad takes his life in his hands because the burden of proof he must meet is so high with today's skeptical voter.

In his 1990 reelection campaign as Arkansas governor, Bill Clinton saved his political career with a rebuttal ad. In the final days of the race, Sheffield Nelson, Clinton's Republican opponent, ran an ad using Clinton's own voice saying the words "raise and spend" to emphasize the taxes Clinton had raised as governor. "What did he do to us in 1979?" the ad asked. "Raise and spend," Clinton's voice answered. "And what did he do to us in 1983?" it asked again. "Raise and spend" the voice replied. "And what will he do to us next year if we reelect him?" "Raise and spend."

By the Saturday before the Tuesday election, Clinton had fallen nine points and was staring defeat in the face. Hurriedly, he drove to his TV taping studio at 2:00 A.M. on Sunday morning to tape his rebuttal. Catching his opponent in a lie, Clinton made the most of it. His ad read,

> You've probably heard the negative commercial Sheffield Nelson is running using my own voice to say I'll raise taxes. Well, in my speech to the legislature two years ago, I said, "Unlike Washington, which can write a check on an account that is overdrawn, we can't. In Arkansas, we have to raise and spend, or we can't spend." I was pushing for a balanced budget, not urging higher taxes. But Nelson got his scissors and cut out the words "raise and spend"

on the tape to give you the wrong impression. You just can't trust Sheffield Nelson.

The effect was immediate. Nelson dropped fast and Clinton regained his lead, winning by eight points.

A candidate's record in areas like taxes, defense, or crime is hard to grasp, often very complex, and frequently contradictory. A negative ad that attacks the past record of a candidate is no match for a rebuttal that seizes on a misrepresentation made over the TV that very night by one of the candidates. You are seeing misrepresentation and prevarication right in front of you. The candidate is caught, seemingly red-handed. The more complex the distortion, the more its unraveling makes good TV.

Too often, campaign managers and their media gurus will not answer opposition attacks, saying that, in doing so, they are ceding control of the dialogue to the adversary's issue. Particularly among Republicans, there is an almost religious aversion to rebuttals. They see answering negatives as the equivalent of a turtle flipping over on its back, defenseless, belly-up. "We're playing into their hands," a consultant will typically say about running a rebuttal ad.

But the price of ignoring a negative ad can be high. Senator Ben Nighthorse Campbell of Colorado defeated Terry Considine, a brilliant, able Republican, because Considine didn't answer Campbell's negative ad. Considine was nursing a hard-won, four-point lead going into the final week. Campbell's brilliant adman, Joe Slade White of Buffalo, ran a negative commercial criticizing Considine for "not paying his property taxes." It was a simple and devastating shot.

The facts, however, were a bit more complex. Considine was a real-estate maven who took over properties where the owner had defaulted and turned them around with sound management, a kind of real-estate relief pitcher. Hired by a bank to turn around a defaulted property, he made it work and began making mortgage and tax payments to the bank that had brought him in. Unfortunately, the bank, Silverado Savings and Loan, went broke and didn't pass the property taxes on to the government. When sued for the taxes, Considine countered that he'd already paid them. He ultimately won on appeal in court, but lost in the election.

Considine's campaign manager vetoed any rebuttal ad. "You'll never explain the facts in thirty seconds," he said. "Even if you do, all you'll have done is deny the allegation. How will that help us win the election?"

But he was wrong. The Campbell negative very well could have been answered in thirty seconds. Listen up:

> *Have you ever gotten one of those annoying phone calls, where they self-righteously demand that you pay a debt or pay your taxes? Aren't they especially annoying when you've actually paid them already? Well, now you know how Terry Considine feels. He has to watch, every night, a negative ad by Ben Nighthorse Campbell saying that Considine didn't pay his taxes. But he did. Here's a copy of the check. And here's the court decision saying it was all he owed. If campbell can't get his facts straight in an ad, how will he ever get them straight in the senate?*

But the ad never ran. If it had, well . . .

Anytime your opponent hits you with a negative ad, cheer up. It's a glorious opportunity to catch him in a misstatement or falsehood. Even if the actual facts he cites are true, but the implication really isn't, you can nail him.

Dole tried to distort Clinton's record on immigration by running an ad showing footage of thousands running to the United States through the border gate marked MEXICO. The ad accused Clinton of wanting to protect "benefits" for illegal aliens. The fact is that the president opposed any welfare or other entitlements for illegals, but did feel that they shouldn't be thrown out of schools. The GOP had called education a "benefit" for the benefit of making a dubious point in its ad.

However, since Clinton's polling showed the public about evenly split on the issue of kicking children of illegal immigrants out of public schools, he decided not to pounce on the inaccuracy. But Clinton did rip Dole on his charge that the president had done little to keep out illegal immigrants. The Democratic rebuttal ad noted that the administration had doubled the number of border guards, sharply increased deportations, and favored cutoff of all aid to illegal aliens.

But each rebuttal ad is just a setup for the main event, the counterpunch. Here is the golden chance to go negative, without any backlash, by attacking your opponent while rebutting his charges. The rebuttal scores all the points a negative ad would have but without the stigma of being negative.

So, the Clinton immigration-ad response went on to note that Dole had voted against establishing a drug czar and had opposed toughening sanctions against employers who hire illegal immigrants. The Dole ad, designed to turn California from a solid Clinton state to a toss-up, did nothing and fell flat, killed by a rebuttal.

It was amazing how Dole's campaign continued to run an attack ad long after Clinton's people had put up a rebuttal that blew it out of the water. The polling and focus groups showed that the Clinton ad had beat the Dole ad, but week after week, the Dole campaign would stay with the discredited ad on the air. It became increasingly clear that the ads were backfiring as voters saw the rebuttal, and that the ads were costing Dole points rather than gaining him any. But the ads stayed on. Republicans usually answer a negative ad with another negative. This "so's your mother" strategy doesn't tap the huge potential of the rebuttal ad. But how do you train an elephant?

Some elephants don't need training. The turning point in Congressman Trent Lott's ascension to the U.S. Senate came when his Democratic opponent, Wayne Dowdy, ran an attack ad featuring a Lott look-alike who rode in the back of a limousine, which hurtled past a mailbox where an old lady was anxiously seeking her Social Security check. "Let's cut Trent Lott's chauffeur and preserve Social Security benefits instead," the ad concluded.

It turned out that the facts were not quite the way Dowdy was presenting them. Lott's highly successful rebuttal featured the chauffeur himself, a late-middle-aged African-American man named George Awkard, saying,

> *For twenty-five years I've served on the Washington, D.C., Police Force and most recently on the detail assigned to Capitol Hill. After the terrorist bombing of the U.S. Capitol, Congress voted to protect its leaders and my job has been to be Congressman Trent Lott's bodyguard. Now Wayne Dowdy is running a negative ad in Mississippi saying that I'm Trent Lott's chauffeur. Mr. Dowdy, I'm nobody's chauffeur: Got it?*

Sometimes you come upon a rebuttal ad just aching to be made.

If You Must Go Negative

If you can't find anything better to say, then you might as well go negative. If you do, remember that any political attack consists of two key elements: impact and credibility. For the ad to work, it has to pack a punch, incite voter outrage, and be credible even in the face of an opposition rebuttal. Negative ads that fail usually stress impact, not credibility.

Impact and credibility are often inversely related. Ads that have high impact, with slamming jail doors and cowering old ladies on dark streets, lack credibility because they require that the voter have no repect at all for the object of the ads' attack.

In 1988, Cleveland's Republican Mayor George Voinivitch was locked in a close race with the Democratic incumbent, U.S. Senator Howard Metzenbaum. In the last month of the race, Voinivitch's advertising firm ran a negative commercial attacking Metzenbaum for a vote opposing the expansion of federal authority to prosecute child pornographers. Voinivitch's ad shredded Metzenbaum for being soft on child pornography and spoke of the Republican's determination to be tougher.

Voters hated the ad. They knew that Metzenbaum probably had opposed the law out of his concern for civil liberties, but the ad made it seem that he was coddling child pornographers. Metzenbaum may be too liberal, Ohio voters figured, but he's not *in favor* of child pornography. He's not *that* bad. When Metzenbaum ran his rebuttal, the firestorm knocked Voinivitch out of contention. He came back two years later to run successfully for governor and recently got his seat in the Senate, but he had hired a new advertising firm.

The key in negative advertising is to produce a credible commercial. If the merits of the issue are sufficiently salient, a relatively bland and nonpartisan statement of the facts will be enough to elicit a strong reaction. The ad must be so believable that it wins the struggle with skepticism that rages in the mind of each voter.

When New Mexico Democrat Jeff Bingaman opposed incumbent Republican Senator Jack Schmidt in 1984, he faced a tough predicament. Schmidt had an 80 percent popularity rating and he was a national hero, having walked on the moon. Obviously, a straight negative ad wouldn't work. Attacking Schmidt would have been the equivalent of spitting on Superman's cape.

The polling showed that New Mexico's environmentally conscious electorate passionately opposed opening national wilderness areas and parks to oil exploration. Schmidt backed the idea, while Bingaman opposed it. Rather than attack Schmidt's position and motivation with vigor and vitriol, linking his vote to the oil-company contributions he had received, Bingaman chose to run the fairest comparative ad possible. Produced by media genius Tony Schwartz, the ad read,

> *Do you think oil companies should be allowed to drill in national parks and wilderness areas? Senator Jack Schmidt says they should because we need the oil. Jeff Bingaman says they shouldn't because no matter how much we may need the oil, we need to protect our heritage more. It's a tough question and the two good men running for senate disagree. On election day, vote for the one who agrees with you.*

The very impartiality of the ad strengthened its credibility and therefore, its ultimate impact. Bingaman still serves in the Senate, a beneficiary of one of the most polite and effective negative ads ever run.

Voters detest negative ads because they look and sound seamy. Their very tone and style shrieks yellow journalism and sensationalism. The ads seem almost to bet to be disbelieved. In Mississippi, voters do not approve of negative ads. "We don't speak ill of our neighbors," a member of Republican Congressman Trent Lott's staff told me, as we planned his race for the U.S. Senate in 1988. Lott, the future Republican Senate majority leader faced, a tough fight against Democratic Congressman Wayne Dowdy. How could we raise the issue of Dowdy's terrible attendance record without offending delicate Mississippi sensibilities?

The media firm of Robert and Adam Goodman produced beautiful, evocative positive ads with little zingers in each one. One featured a teenage girl who spoke enthusiastically of Trent Lott's assistance in getting her an electric wheelchair so she could attend classes at Ole Miss. As she zipped around the campus, the announcer noted that, by the way, Wayne Dowdy had missed the vote to allocate these funds, but it was okay, because Trent Lott was there and he made sure the bill passed anyway. By dropping the negative in an almost offhanded way, we minimized the backlash among the voters.

A negative campaign is most prone to backfire when it is the candidate himself who leads the attack. Harry Truman did an inestimable disservice to politics by popularizing the notion that the public likes a feisty candidate who "gives 'em hell." They don't. Voters feel such candidates are irresponsible, negative windbags who don't have a clue and so spend their time attacking their opponents.

There is a vast difference between negative ads that attack the character or personal integrity of one's opponent and those that contrast issue positions that are fairly in the public sector. Ad hominum attacks almost never work. But the public regards issue comparisons not as negative but as informational and comparative. The more generous the ads are in describing the motivations and details of the opponent's position, the more credible—and the more effective—they will be.

CHAPTER 35

Paid Advertising: An End Run Around the Media

D OES THE MEDIA have a life-and-death power over candidacies? Are the barons of TV, radio, and the press the new political bosses, able to elect and defeat people at will?

No.

The crucial difference between the media's power over government and its more limited role in politics is paid advertising. Candidates can advertise and speak directly to voters, bypassing the filter of media coverage. Voters, appreciate the information this direct communication provides. Suspicious of both ads and journalists, they use one to check out the bias and accuracy of the other.

Press secretaries are forever trying to protect the candidate in the press. They closely watch what their man says and coach him on the spin and the needs of each reporter. But many press aides ignore the equally important goal of protecting the campaign's advertising from negative comments by the press.

When you run an ad, provide extensive documentation for each sentence and every assertion. Make sure the thirty-second ad is backed up by a brief, with clippings from the Congressional Record included. Find out who is going to "review" your ad for the local papers and go through an endless interview to defend each comma in the ad. Better, go through this process twice—once before you issue the ad, in a rehearsal, and once after it is out. Anything you can't defend, don't put on the air.

The press tends to regard paid media as a hostile intrusion on its monopoly in conveying political information to voters. They watch the reality, not the television. Voters watch the television. Until the media links its political coverage more directly to political advertising, it will lose much of its potential power in shaping electoral outcomes.

Journalists generally don't do a very good job of covering the paid advertising. They tend to focus their coverage on the candidates themselves as they campaign, shake hands, give speeches, or conduct interviews. This coverage is crucial, since it is the candidate who will become governor or senator. But it ignores the role the media should play in refereeing the advertising to keep it honest. The press needs to expand its role in monitoring advertising so that it is a fair umpire of the process.

Most media publishes reviews of the ads almost as if the ads were movies, but these reviews tend to be buried in the paper and rarely are written in a decisive enough style to make a difference. They are usually written in an "on the one hand, on the other hand" style.

The impact of media in elections varies depending on the office at issue. Generally, races for the Senate and the House are poorly covered by the media. While the media exercises a crucial role in presidential campaigns, it rarely is the deciding force in races for Congress.

The Washington bureaus of the local papers are too focused on keeping up with national stories to spend much time covering the doings and votes of their hometown senators or congresspeople. In these contests, advertising is the key.

In races for governor when the state capital is also the major city (such as Boston, Denver, Indianapolis, or Little Rock), media coverage of a gubernatorial race tends to be very intense. But in states where the capital is in a smaller town (e.g., Albany, Harrisburg, Springfield, or Sacramento), the coverage of a run for governor is rarely on the front page in the major media markets of the state. Mayoral races, by contrast, are always heavily covered by the media, usually by a highly experienced City Hall press corps.

In handling the press during a campaign, the key point is to realize that every news outlet slants every story every time to achieve objectives that go well beyond the news. This is not usually yellow journalism, it is just the media doing what it sees as its job. In the most venal cases, the media will always harness their coverage to ideological goals to reward some politicians who curry their favor and destroy those who don't.

But even in responsible news organs, each reporter has his own bias. Rarely is it ideological or partisan. Usually, it is based on the reporter's personal experiences with politicians and his or her inclination toward cynicism or toward credulity. It's very important to grasp the individual bias of each reporter. While voters see newspapers or TV stations, politicians must see each individual reporter as his or her own media outlet, separate from the others.

When you promote a story to a reporter, have other sources prepped with quotes to back you up and provide one-stop shopping for all the data the journalist needs. When a journalist is going to interview your candidate, work hard to find out what is on his or her mind. Read his other stories and prepare your candidate thoroughly.

All media is hostage to ratings. What the voters want to see and hear, networks and newspapers have to carry. The best way to secure positive coverage is to use advertising—paid media—to influence the public which, in turn, influences how the news media covers events. By running ads attacking the Republican budget cuts of 1995, Clinton helped trigger massive hostility to Gingrich's Contract With America. When news shows interviewed average citizens, they got an earful, blistering Gingrich and Dole. This structured their coverage and led to the declaration that Clinton had "won" the budget fight and that the public "blamed" the GOP for the government shutdown.

In handling newspapers with an editorial bias against you, work off them to appeal to your constituency. The *Boston Globe*'s liberalism is well known in Massachusetts. When conservative Ed King defeated liberal Mike Dukakis in 1978, the *Globe*'s opposition to King served to ratify his claims to being a sincere, anti-tax conservative. If the *Globe* knocked King, lots of blue-collar conservatives thought more of him. Similarly, Democrats running for president in the New Hampshire primary work hard to earn the animus of the *Manchester Union Leader*, the notoriously right-wing newspaper, in order to seal their liberal credentials with the Democratic primary electorate.

By playing off the editorial boards, you can convince your own constituency of your ideological sincerity. If they hate you, you must be doing something right.

CHAPTER 36

How to Win if You Are Zero Charisma

T HERE IS NO UNIFORM TYPE of charisma. This elusive combination of attractiveness and chemistry is a quality that expands and changes as each new popular political leader creates his own form of charisma.

The Kennedy fixation of American voters has tended to stylize one type of charisma—young, handsome, sleek, and elegant—as the only variety. Not so. Just as charisma is an indefinable attraction, so its forms are infinitely varied. The underlying requisite for charisma is not some mystical attractiveness, but rather that voters agree with you and like what you are trying to do. Once there is a basic empathy with your purpose, direction, and policies, voters will seek out your quirks and eccentricities and declare them to be charismatic.

Harry Truman seemed small in every way as he succeeded FDR. Instead of the rich, charismatic, mellow voice of Roosevelt, heard over fireside chats on radios throughout America, Truman had a harsh, high-pitched nasal twang. Small in both physical and political stature, this former haberdasher seemed the opposite of FDR. But as Truman gained popularity, his feistiness, aggressiveness, willingness to speak plainly, and his tendency to "give 'em hell" endeared him to voters. A new form of charisma attached itself to his personality.

Eisenhower's smile and avuncular manner became its own form of charisma. The opposite of Kennedy's youth and dash, Eisenhower's friendly likability showed in his famous grin and was mirrored in his slogan, "I Like Ike."

Who would have thought that a president well into his seventies would be seen as charismatic? Through the spectrum of Kennedy charisma, Ronald Reagan's Everyman popularity is inexplicable. Yet when the assassin's bullet missed his heart, Reagan's quips, his calm self-assurance, his fervent hope that the doctors were Republicans, created a charismatic following for him. His jauntiness, ironic twist of phrase, and witty common sense made him irresistible to the average voter.

Even George Bush became charismatic when he stood up to Saddam Hussein. His high-pitched, geeky, whining voice no longer sounded like nails scratching a blackboard. It came to remind Americans of a Yankee preacher holding firm against sin. His breeding did not suggest, as it once had, that he was, in Ann Richards' immortal phrase, "born with a silver foot in his mouth." No, now it showed a patrician firmness and a well-tempered calm under fire. Barbara Bush, "his grandmother" as people said in 1988, was now charming, understated, real, and Yankee.

Few saw Clinton as charismatic before his 1996 reelection. Voters thought he was fleshy, self-indulgent, verbose, unctuous, overly solicitous, and anxious to be ingratiating. But charismatic? No. But by 1996, he had developed his own charisma. His empathy, dignity under fire, and tall, stately bearing replaced the plump man in jogging shorts in our collective consciousness. His garrulous, chatty, endless speeches, rivaling Fidel Castro's in length, no longer were deadening or boring. Voters came to see them as a model of rationality, the first time anyone had bothered to explain, simply and slowly, about the global economy and our response to it.

How much of the inability of Johnson, Nixon, Ford, or Carter to acquire charisma was due to their personality and how much to their lack of popularity? Early in his terms, Johnson's oversized Texas personality seemed attractive as he draped his long arms around senators to cajole their votes for civil rights. Nixon's small-town humility and earnestness seemed attractive at the start of his term amid the tortured intellectualism of the New Left on college campuses. Gerry Ford's lack of guile initially seemed very alluring after the chicanery of the Nixon years. Carter's grin, his honest sincerity, and his lack of pomposity were charismatic as he campaigned in 1976.

But ultimately, it was Johnson's crude insensitivity, Nixon's paranoid corruption, Ford's bumbling inability, and Carter's over-matched ineptitude that came to dominate their images. This is more because they failed to attract voters with their policies than that they lacked charisma. Had their programs and ideas kept their ratings high, charisma would have followed. It's like the old song: "She's got yellow teeth. Now I never cared for yellow teeth, but she's got yellow teeth and that's my weakness now."

Unpopular politicians who are clearly charismatic find that their very charisma operates as a negative, leaving them to seem hollow, an empty suit, the facade of attraction with nothing inside. Consider how Dan Quayle's blond good looks came to be derided as the "deer-caught-in-the-headlights stare." Many an attractive female candidate has been attacked as "Betty Boop" or an "airhead." In 1969, as the snow piled up and the plows broke down, voters in Queens, New York, came to see the lean, athletic frame of Mayor John V. Lindsay as a callow, youthful incompetent, in over his pretty little head. Snow will do that to a mayor. After Donna Rice, Gary Hart probably wanted to hide his good looks under a bushel. He would have survived more easily had he been old and frumpy.

Charisma is the most elusive of political traits because it doesn't exist in reality, only in our perception once a candidate has made it by hard work and good issues.

So, let all potential candidates stop practicing in front of full-length mirrors. Don't opine to your hairdresser to give you that Kennedy look or ask your speech coach about adopting a downward chopping hand motion. Bald candidates need not despair. There may even be as yet unproven charisma in obesity, wrinkles, and double chins. Take heart.

CHAPTER 37

California Dreamin':
Winning Issue Referenda

MORE AND MORE of America's crucial political issues will not be decided by our elected senators, congressmen, legislators, or even presidents. The movement toward making fundamental decisions through direct voter participation is irreversible and fundamental. For anybody who wants to influence substantive outcomes in our political process, it will become more essential with each year that they master the referenda process.

Winning a referendum is nothing at all like winning an election for a candidate. The most basic difference is that voters who elect a person know what they are getting, for the most part. If you vote for Clinton and he wins, Clinton becomes president. One may wonder what he is really like or what he will do after he wins, but at least his physical body and mind will occupy the Oval Office.

With a ballot issue, you never know what you will get if it is enacted. The words on the piece of paper can be interpreted by judges, sheriffs, prosecutors, or legislators as they wish. Nobody can be completely sure what a "yes" vote will mean.

Most people looking at an issue referendum assume that the contest will be based on the arguments for or against the question on the ballot. But that's wrong. The contest usually boils down to a battle of interpretation of what the amendment or proposition will do if it is passed.

For example, almost every poll conducted in the 1970s and 1980s indicated that two-thirds of the American people supported the Equal Rights Amendment (ERA), which would have banned sexual discrimination. But the ERA was defeated in a large number of states, including in liberal New York state. Polls indicated that even as the ERA was being defeated, it still enjoyed a strong majority of public support.

But the ERA lost because its opponents reinterpreted its simple provisions to suggest that they would require women to go into combat or eliminate gender distinctions in restrooms. By inventing any kind of wild fantasy about what the ERA intended, adversaries were able to distract the debate from issues like equal pay or non-discrimination into phobic concerns that derailed the amendment.

The list of good proposals that have been defeated by being misinterpreted is depressing and extensive. Gun controls were rejected in Massachusetts because voters were worried that police could search houses for weapons. The bottle bill was beaten in Washington state after opponents succeeded in portraying a refundable deposit as a tax increase. The tobacco industry recently killed anti-smoking legislation by enlisting voter sympathy for the poor working people who would have to pay more in taxes for their habit if the legislation were enacted. Reforms of very high union pay-scales for public construction in Massachusetts were rejected because opponents succeeded in getting voters to confuse the idea of a "prevailing wage" with "minimum wage."

Time and again, zealous advocates of good causes have lost because they were not sufficiently careful in drafting their initiatives or in titling how they would appear on the ballot. Similarly, bad guys have very often gotten referenda passed by selling them falsely to the voters.

In California, the drive to repeal affirmative action cloaked itself in the garment of civil rights by wording its ballot language to bar discrimination or preferences based on race or gender. While the effect was to kill affirmative-action preferences for minorities and women, the language implied that the "yes" vote was a strike in favor of civil rights as they have been traditionally defined.

In defeating bad ballot propositions, the key is to strike at the interpretation likely to follow the adoption of the statute. When liberals tried to defeat the California initiative that banned state aid to illegal immigrants, they argued that it was important to provide a good education to every member of the community, even those that were here illegally. But when a media firm proposed a TV ad showing storm troopers, in full metal jackets, invading a public school, lining up the children, checking identification, and carting off the crying children of illegal immigrants, the ad was judged too hot to handle. The liberals lost.

Because so much of the fate of a ballot proposition is tied up in its language and how it will be used if passed, support or opposition are notoriously volatile. A ballot issue does not have the residual history of trust that a candidate usually enjoys to allay fears of what mendacity might follow its victory. Any interpretation, no matter how farfetched, needs to be taken seriously. Who knows how some judge might interpret the language twenty or thirty years from now?

Unlike a candidate, a ballot proposition cannot look sincerely into the camera and assure voters of his intentions and motivation. It must stand or fall on the text and its interpretation. It is there that the real battle for its passage or defeat is waged.

Sometimes, special interests try to pass a ballot issue by concealing from the general public that it is on the ballot. In a famous case in the mid-1980s, labor unions won a key ballot fight by resisting all invitations to advertise on television or to debate the question in public. Instead, they waged a stealth campaign to reach union members and keep the general level of public interest in the issue as low as possible.

In virtually every ballot-issue fight, corporate interests can outspend public-interest advocates. To offset this advantage, one must use jujitsu—make the enemy's strength work against him. A good move is to use an opponent's donors against him. By revealing that the other side is funded by polluters or other bad guys, one can often carry the day. Once a donor list is attacked, the ballot issue acquires an image and a personality all its own. The issue is no longer just an abstract question appearing on a voting machine, but becomes perceived as a power grab by the corporations or interest groups that are promoting it.

When facing an adversary who can outspend you 3-to-1 or worse, the key is to use his advertising to frame your message. In Washington state in the early 1980s, environmental forces sought to curb nuclear power's growth. They hit upon an idea marvelous in its simplicity and impact—require a voter referendum before bonds could be issued for a nuclear-power project. The well-funded nuclear industry launched a massive TV campaign to defeat the proposition, featuring a worried taxpayer adding up on his calculator the cost of all the environmental-impact statements and referenda required by the initiative. The environmentalists could only afford ads ten seconds in length in the last ten days before the election. But it did the trick. The ads showed a split screen with a voter in a polling place on one side of the screen and a giant nuclear power plant on the other. The announcer said, "What costs more? Holding an election or building a nuclear power plant?" The environmentalists won.

CHAPTER 38

How to Tame Your Political Consultants

F EWER THAN FORTY political consultants handle over three-quarters of the well-funded major campaigns in the United States. Evenly divided between the political parties, they are the professionals of the process. Their power rivals that of the old-time political bosses. Intensely competitive, they frequently work on the same side in one state and against each other, at the same time, in another. Like bees pollinating a garden, they carry strategies from one place to the next. When one of them comes up with a new issue or innovative tactic, all the others watch intently. If it succeeds, they imitate it and soon the idea makes its way throughout the country.

To the voter, the election contest is between candidates. To the political parties, it is Democrats against Republicans. But to the consultants, the contests usually boil down to fights between one another. In bars and on planes, they will be heard to say, "I beat so-and-so in Kansas. Now I'm up against him in Florida." The name they'll use isn't the defeated candidate, but his consultant.

While both parties use consultants for polling and for media, Republicans tend to add a layer: the general consultant. Regardless of the titles, in each campaign there is usually one consultant who runs the show. By virtue of his or her closer relationship with the candidate or manager, or simply by force of reputation or personality, the campaign usually pivots around a single advisor, pollster, or media consultant or generalist.

Some consultants, particularly many pollsters, are simply vending machines. You insert your money and out comes polling data without much analysis or creativity. They see themselves as disinterested auditors of a corporation's books. They come in without a vested interest in one strategy or another and examine what's working and what isn't. If you hire one of these consultants, you better make sure somebody else is providing the creativity, because they sure won't be.

Other consultants are prima donnas—the strategists. There are about ten men and women in each party who are true strategists. Among them, they run most of the major political campaigns in the country. They are very good. Constantly learning from their mistakes, they keep abreast of the latest tactics, strategies, technologies, and issues. Apart from the innate merit of the candidate, the adequacy of his funding, and the national party trends at work, it is their insights that make the difference between winning and losing.

The key to getting the best work out of them is to make them listen to your unique views, issues, attributes, and personality. Many consultants almost seem to carry around a cardboard model of what they want the candidate to be. Your job is supposed to be to just put your face in the hole and pose for a picture. Make your consultant *listen to you.* Make him understand what is different about your candidacy and insist that he shape a strategy that is uniquely yours, not a cookie-cutter campaign he is using all over the country.

Some consultants can win only if their candidate is ideologically polarized. Some consultants are only really successful on behalf of conservatives, while others only know how to win from the left side of the spectrum. They are not like battle tanks, endlessly maneuverable, able to shift from one direction to another to meet any attacker. Instead, they tend to be like fixed pieces of artillery, deadly to anyone in range in front of them but unable to swing around to meet an attack from any other direction. If you are comfortable with their ideological mold, you would be well advised to work with them. If not, don't hire one of them because they will always try to push you to the right or the left so you can fit into their paradigm.

Among media creators, fear the artiste who is more determined to win prizes than elections. Beautiful, evocative media does not always do better than plain, ordinary print on the screen. Sometimes, it does a lot worse. Media consultants are forever trying to build up their "reels"—the collection of ads they take to potential clients to pitch business. They often use your campaign budget to subsidize extravagant production values to make the ads look good to the next customer or the film critic, but not to the voter. Travelogues masquerading as advertisements don't get anyone elected.

Don't use checks and balances to hold your consultants under control. In 1996, Dole was forever changing consultants and pitting one against another to keep them in control. The result was total chaos. The campaign had no continuity and lurched from one strategy to the next as heads rolled and new consultants were hired. Don't hire people whose job it is to stop your best consultant from doing his job. Multiple views yield multiple strategies, and that never works. Never.

Hold on to your wallet when you deal with consultants. Make them articulate their fees using dollars, not percentages. In commercial advertising, agencies usually demand a commission arrangement, but in political campaigns, always seek to avoid paying a percentage, just pay a flat fee. Fees negotiated in dollar denominations are always less costly than those articulated as a percentage of the total amount of media purchased.

The key problem with almost all political consultants is that they don't know anything about issues. They focus entirely on tactics, ads, and strategies and learn little about the substance of public policy. As a result, their advice tends to be stereotypical, pushing the issue du jour that has worked in another state. They suggest rounding up the usual suspects when formulating a campaign's issues and rarely try to come up with new or creative formulations. Most consultants are too timid to venture outside of the normal orbit of political issues, yet it is precisely there that you will find the best ways to win.

In dealing with your consultant, insist on his personal presence during the race. Conference calls are no substitute for making him visit your headquarters and spend the entire day learning what is happening in your race. Consultants are anxious to work in as many campaigns as possible. While this is understandable from their professional perspective, it often undermines their ability to give enough attention to each race. The variant is how often they come. You would be well advised to key their compensation to the frequency of their visits. When their body is in your headquarters, their mind usually follows.

The Irrelevance of the Undecided Voter

MOST PUNDITS STROKE their chins in the hours before the polls close and speculate on who will get the "undecided" vote. Few questions are less important. Mythically, undecided voters are the most serious students of the process, reserving their judgment until all the facts are in; they make up their minds as they enter the voting booth. In reality, undecided voters usually don't know or care who's running and are most likely not to vote at all. Ross Perot's appeal in 1992 rested on his ability to make many of these non-voters participate. But, barring an eccentric candidacy like Perot or Jesse "The Body" Ventura, Minnesota's Reform Party governor, few undecided voters ever actually make it to the polls in a typical contest.

Obviously, at the start of an election campaign, most voters are undecided because they haven't heard of the candidates before. But as the campaign matures and candidates get better known, the voters who are left undecided are usually those who don't care and can't be bothered. When candidates gain or lose points during a campaign, the votes rarely come from the undecideds. One candidate's gain is usually his opponent's loss. The undecided vote tends to remain relatively constant.

When undecided voters don't stay home, they usually vote against the incumbent. An uncommitted person has usually decided not to vote for the incumbent; he just hasn't learned the name of the other candidate yet. In the presidential races between 1960 and 1996, more than nine undecideds out of ten who actually voted ended up backing the challenger and opposing the incumbent. Even such benighted campaigns as those of Barry Goldwater, George McGovern, and Walter Mondale managed to pick up the bulk of the undecided vote on election day.

In the preelection polls of 1996, Clinton generally led by thirteen to fifteen points, yet his election day margin shrank to nine. In this case, predictably, the undecided vote went to the challenger Bob Dole. Clinton's big mistake was not including Independent Ross Perot in the candidate debates. Clinton urged Perot's inclusion but didn't insist on it when the Candidate Debate Commission ruled against including the third-party challenger. The president should have boycotted the debates unless Perot was included. If Perot had debated, he probably would have absorbed most of the undecided vote as he had in 1992, increasing Clinton's margin over Dole and likely carrying Congress for the Democrats.

Clinton let Perot be excluded because he was fearful of having to debate him. He was glad to be able to debate Dole and slaughter him; Perot would have complicated things. But Perot's exclusion from the debates sent a signal that he wasn't a serious contender, and he finished with only half the vote he got in 1992, while Dole walked off with the undecideds.

So, don't worry about the undecideds. If you are an incumbent, you'll never get them anyway, and if there is no incumbent, they'll never vote in any large numbers.

Instead, work to switch those who say they are voting for your opponent to your side—that's where the action is.

CHAPTER 40

If You Are on a Staff: How to Handle Your Boss

NEVER TAKE AN APPOINTED position from a politician unless you have your own power base. Having a source of strength outside the control of the person who appoints you is the difference between employment and slavery in working for a politician.

Your power can come from good relationships with legislators or congressmen, friendships with reporters, support from parts of the district, access to important contributors, a nexus with special-interest groups, even from knowledge of a specialized field the elected official needs to know about. But those who serve only "at the pleasure" of their boss, with no power base, are no better than feudal serfs.

If you take an appointed position, your first task is to carve out your own power base so that you can function and survive. Do your day job and then work assiduously to cultivate your own sources of political strength. Until you locate a potential reservoir of support and begin to tap it, you are on probation, hanging by a thread.

Indeed, a staffer really isn't of much use to a politician unless he has a power base. With a limited number of staff slots, an elected official needs to use each one to cultivate a source of support. What is a power base to you, is an opportunity to your boss.

Power in politics is thrust upon the staff member. Influence peddlers, who cannot have access to the top man, work hard to influence and empower the people they can reach. If they can't be with the one they love, they love the one they're with. Lobbyists, political supporters, donors, and even press people do their utmost to help a staff member maximize his influence and power. Since they count on his future gratitude, they feel the investment in the staff member's future is worthwhile. They work to build up a staff member's power by feeding him information. Money is no longer "the mother's milk of politics." Information is. The lobbyists and influence peddlers will say, confidentially, "Your boss may want to know . . . " or "Did you hear what Congressman so-and-so is doing?" or "You might want to call Mr. X, I think you could get a contribution out of him." They know that by sharing information, they are helping to maximize your value to your boss, your power. The more influence you have, the more influence they have through you.

In serving on a staff, specialize as quickly as possible. Take an issue or a role and make it yours. Don't wait for instructions. As Plunkett of Tammany Hall once said, "See your opportunities and take 'em." Look around the office and develop your own product of which you become the sole source supplier. Jacks-of-all-trades are doomed to diminishment and dismissal.

Are you the one who knows about trade issues? Do you have a good contact at Social Security to help with constituent service? Is your best friend the head of the neighborhood association in part of the district? Are you the best writer? Can you repair the fax machine? Anything for a role, a function, and a base.

In Congress, there is a subculture of staff members who operate according to their own rules. Like monkeys climbing a tree, they swing from branch to branch—job to job—moving up. First, they rise from the constituent-service job, usually the lowest rung on a congressman's staff, to the top slot, administrative assistant. Thence, they go from one AA job to another, moving up the congressional pecking order as they work for increasingly influential congressmen. Finally, they reach the top of the tree and become chief of staff to a standing committee. At the zenith of their power, these unknown, unelected people have enormous clout. They dominate the cabinet department they oversee and tend to remain in power for decades, watching presidents and cabinets come and go, while they remain serenely supreme.

The key to mastering upward mobility on congressional staffs is to adjust to the mood of the body. In the House, a panty-raid psychology predominates. Members get together in ad hoc caucuses to raise hell and attract attention from a usually oblivious Speaker. Like anti-establishment pranksters at a party-oriented college, they form fraternities seeking to prick the power structure and make it move ever so slightly in their direction.

A House staffer should use his access to the staffs of other members to help build bridges for his boss and to bring him information about what's going on. Congressmen are social creatures who must move in herds to survive. Staffers who assist in this process of bonding and group formation can really make a difference for their boss and for themselves.

The Senate is a different story. When Trent Lott moved from the House to the Senate, he noted that dealing with the various senators was like dealing with so many different heads of state. "In the House, you'd go over to a guy on the floor," Lott said, "and say, 'How about voting for my amendment?' The other guy'd look it over and say, 'Makes sense, count me in.' But up here in the Senate, he says, 'I'll think about it. I'll have my people take a look at it.'

Everything is reviewed by the staffs, and the senators lack the spontaneity of House members. It's like dealing with foreign heads of state."

As Senate Majority Leader, Lott has tried to bring some of the House spirit to the Senate, but the institution is hard to move. For staff members, this distance and formality among senators can be daunting. Much more dignity is required. The antics of the House are very different from the decorum of the Senate. Power in the Senate comes through power on an individual senator's staff rather than on the upward movement from staff to staff that characterizes the House. A position as chief of a senator's staff is the top of the pyramid. It is a position of tremendous power. Inside the typical senator's office, power changes hands slowly, as senators tend to stay in office for decades. The best way to get power on a senator's staff is to help get him elected. The second-best way is to wait your turn.

In the White House, there are really two staffs: the president's and the chief of staff's. The chief of staff exerts nominal control over all who work in the White House, but his mandate is limited when he must deal with those who have direct access to the president. Those who work for the chief of staff, on the other hand, need to be careful not to have too much contact with the chief executive, lest the chief of staff feel jealous of their access.

Obviously, it is much better to work for the president than for the chief of staff. The problem is how to make the transition. Unless you enter the White House with a long, close, preexisting relationship with the president, you have to begin by working for his chief of staff or even for the head of your department. The key to survival and success is to get out from under their control as soon as possible and become one of the president's own people.

Here, the key is proximity to the president. Getting a seat on Air Force One and taking advantage of the clubby intimacy of travel with the president is a good way to do this—as is writing speeches or doing scheduling that brings you into direct and frequent contact with the chief executive. Political consultants and fund-raisers enjoy a special and direct access to the president every four years, and congressional-relations people can get that access during times of hot legislative crisis.

In making the transition from the chief of staff's staff to the president's staff, it is crucial not to be too obvious and to make the shift a gradual one. There is a great danger of falling into limbo. Chiefs of staff are used to end runs and work hard at preventing them. The key here is whether the president encourages changes of allegiance. Clinton, Johnson, and FDR always did. Bush, Reagan, and Eisenhower seem not to have shared this style.

Both in the White House and in Congress, some staffers don't seek power in government nearly as much if they really want a stepping stone to power in an outside occupation. A press secretary will use his access to reporters and editors to line up his next job at a newspaper or TV station. Foreign-policy experts will use their entrée to join the Council on Foreign Relations or become active in international finance. Legal counsels will want prestige and position so as to enter a top law firm or to move to the judiciary. Those who oversee an administrative agency for a congressional committee will seek to parlay their access into a lobbying job. The permanent establishments of Washington pick over the executive and congressional staffs in finding their future partners and executives.

The ultimate power of a staff member is the power to resign. Former president of France Charles de Gaulle used resignation as a weapon better than anyone else. "I chose to withdraw from power before power withdrew from me," he said, explaining his resignation as prime minister of postwar France in 1946.

"Pulling a de Gaulle" means getting out while you are on top, before you go back down again. When the power balance in an office has shifted against you, read the handwriting on the wall and get out. Don't threaten resignation unless you mean it. But adjust your mind and your insecurity quotient so that you *can* mean it. A staff member who can quit is a staff member with power. One who is chained to his oar through insecurity is powerless.

In a resignation, you bring the ultimate pressure to bear on a politician. He usually can't risk having you outside as a free agent. You know too much. You have too many contacts. In a resignation, you amass all your power and force your point of view on your boss. If he will listen, you'll un-resign and live happily. If he won't listen, then you know you're on your way out anyway so move on to another opportunity.

CHAPTER 41

Racism Doesn't Work

R ACISM IS INCREASINGLY SPENT as a political force. The 1996 election was one of the first in which race played little or no role. Affirmative action, billed as the new "hot button" in 1995, failed miserably as a tool for demagogues after Clinton defanged the issue by distinguishing it from racial quotas. Even in California, where repeal of affirmative action carried the day, the issue did nothing to impede Clinton's victory. Divisive forces—Republican attempts to stir up anti-immigrant sentiment, the issue of welfare benefits for illegal immigrants, and voter initiatives to require that only English be used in schools and governments—had little real effect.

Americans are turned off by racism. For fifty years, crime, welfare, and the competition for jobs have exacerbated racial tensions, but as welfare rolls have dropped, crime has declined, and unemployment has fallen to the lowest levels in decades, racial animosity has also decreased.

Initially, civil-rights advocates urged "majority minority" districts to assure the election of black congressmen. They insisted that unless a district was 60 percent black, a white candidate would likely win regardless of the issues. Republican National Committee Chairman Lee Atwater was delighted. He pushed hard for "majority minority" seats so that African-American voters would be concentrated in certain districts, leaving white Democrats vulnerable to conservative Republican challenges.

But the Supreme Court intervened and ruled that the ridiculously gerrymandered districts, whose lines bent and strained to pick up black voters, were unconstitutional. Alarmists worried that the redrawn districts would cause wholesale defeat of the newly elected black incumbents. But almost all were reelected even though most had to run in white-majority territory. Race didn't matter nearly as much as the left said it would.

General Colin Powell's incredible national popularity shows how little skin color matters in American politics today. Virginia, with less than a quarter of its voting population black, elected Douglas Wilder as governor in the 1980s. In 1996 in North Carolina, over a third of white voters backed black Democrat Harvey Gantt in his unsuccessful bid to topple Republican Jesse Helms. Republican Congressman J. C. Watts, an African-American, won his seat in Oklahoma in an almost all-white district.

Hispanic candidates have an even easier time of it. Frederico Peña was elected mayor of Denver despite its solid Anglo majority. Most polls showed Henry Cisneros in Texas to be a strong statewide candidate before his scandal, even though Hispanics account for less than a fifth of the Texas vote.

Most of the truly race-conscious ballots cast in America today are cast by African-Americans themselves. Democrats, of either race, can regularly count on over 80 percent of black votes against any white Republican candidate. Only rare Republicans like Governor Christie Whitman of New Jersey win significant black backing.

As a result, African-Americans are basically disenfranchised in America today because they only vote for Democrats. To get political power, blacks must put themselves back in play by voting and running as Republicans. Only if they are up for grabs as an electorate will anybody pay attention to their needs. Republican clients usually ask me to poll among whites only. They're not being racist, they just know that the black vote will go against them, so they don't want to pay for the extra interviews.

No Democratic candidate for whom I have ever worked has ever asked me, in a general election, "How can I win the black vote?" It is assumed. I'm often asked how to increase minority turnout mechanically, but never what issues will appeal to minority voters to win their support. Never.

Democrats treat African-American voters like a golf handicap. In a typical state, assured of 13 percent of the vote by winning the blacks, they go out and campaign in search of the remaining 38 percent they need to win.

Yet, America is ready for black Republicans, as the popularity of both General Colin Powell and J. C. Watts in Oklahoma demonstrates. Minority candidates who break with their ideological masters on the left attract flocks of white voters. African-Americans who speak for their growing middle class (now estimated to be about one-third of the black population) have an instant appeal to whites.

Hispanic-Americans, too, can benefit from breaking away from liberalism. New York City's perennial mayoral candidate, Hispanic Herman Badillo, came close to victory several times by having a tough stance on welfare and promoting English literacy and education standards.

Minority candidates who defy their ethnic masters and Democratic Party orthodoxy by urging tough positions on crime, quotas, welfare, and the like win points for courage and independence among

America's voters. When they contest for votes with white conservatives, they tend to stand out and attract supporters because of the character it takes for them to turn away from the consensus of their leadership.

The time is here for minorities to cross party lines as the swelling black middle class finds ideological affinity in Republican conservative positions. Racism is no longer at the core of the Republican Party. You can't win an election on race anymore in America. Thank the Lord.

CHAPTER 42

Women Candidates: Using the Stereotype to Win

T HE STRATEGIC SITUATION women candidates face is totally different from that which black candidates confront. White voters are either racist or they are not. The minority who are bigots will never vote for an African-American. The majority don't care much about race. By contrast, sexism is far more limited. Relatively few people are still opposed to women in politics. Many more voters of both genders want to see more women elected to office.

But despite this relative lack of sexist bias, a woman has a harder time getting elected than does a black candidate. That's why the Congress is 7 percent black. The percentage is low but relatively proportionate to the 12 percent of blacks in the U.S. population. Only 12 percent of the members of the House and Senate are female, even though women make up 52 percent of our population.

American voters don't dislike women candidates, but they do stereotype them. Men and women, sexists or not, all tend to share the same preconceptions about female candidates. A national survey in 1986 probed the extent of this stereotyping. Pollsters asked voters whether a male candidate or a female one would be more likely to be honest, compassionate, fiscally frugal, pro-defense, pro-education, and tough on crime.

Voters answered that the man would do better on fiscal, defense, and crime issues while the woman would be better in the areas of integrity, compassion, and education. Curiously, it did not matter whether the respondents were men or women nor whether they supported or opposed the Equal Rights Amendment (ERA). All four groups of voters shared the exact same stereotypes about women candidates.

The key in electing a woman is to make the stereotype work for her candidacy, not against it. This means two things:

- reducing the edge the man has on male stereotypical issues
- stressing the importance of female stereotypical issues in the campaign.

Women who run should be Thatcheresque in their positions on crime, taxes, and defense. Iron ladies. But that's not enough. No matter how strongly women take a posture on these issues, men candidates will usually have the advantage. But by closing the gap on the male issues, women candidates can emphasize issues like education, the environment, integrity, and other spheres where the female stereotype helps rather than hurts. By making the election turn on these issues, they can win.

Bob Squier, the Democratic media consultant who consulted on the campaign advertisements for President Clinton's campaign in 1996, helped William Winter, his candidate for governor of Mississippi, defeat his female opponent by shooting an ad that reminded voters that the governor was in charge of the state's national guard. By posing his candidate surrounded by soldiers and tanks, he used gender stereotypes to defeat Winter's opponent, Evelyn Gandy.

In 1980, Paula Hawkins was elected to the Senate from Florida, becoming the first woman to sit in that body whose political career was not based on her husband's or father's public achievements. She won her seat by using the gender stereotype to aid her candidacy. On Florida's Public Utility Commission, she first attracted public attention by fighting for consumers. Once elected to the Senate, she sustained her popularity by focusing on issues like child abuse and missing children. Only her poor performance in a 1986 debate, due in part to medical problems, blocked her bid for reelection.

Women must "hug" male opponents—by agreeing with them—on issues that favor men while drawing sharp distinctions from them on issues that help women.

Republicans always supposed that their pro-life position on abortion caused the gender gap to widen in Clinton's favor in 1996. Undoubtedly, it played a role. But Clinton's differences with the Republicans on education policy, gun control, and family-leave laws were far more important in bringing him a disproportionate share of the female vote.

The Republican Party is in danger of acquiring a reputation for opposing public education. Their advocacy of funding cuts, opposition to federally mandated higher standards, and support for the voucher system all lead women to suspect that the GOP would like to see private and parochial schools predominate.

The Republican Party needs to develop its own agenda for reforming public schools. Abolition of teacher tenure—a view the teacher's unions won't let Democrats embrace—could be the cornerstone of a GOP comeback on the public-education issue. This could be the key to closing the gender gap.

CHAPTER 43

Debates: Dominating the Dialogue

P OLITICAL DEBATING has as little to do with the science of debate being practiced in high schools and colleges across America as military music has to do with classical music. A good way to do well in a political debate, if you were a member of your debating team in school, is to forget everything you learned and start again.

A political debate between candidates is about ratifying *your* issues and *the* issues in the campaign and looking good on camera while doing so. It is not about defeating your adversary's arguments, proving your case, or—least of all—answering the questions reporters put to you.

When the candidates square off in the thick of the campaign, the debate is really a chance for each campaign's issue schematic to go up against that of the opposition, to see which is more worthy of public focus. It is the content of the debate, more than the performance of its participants, that will determine the winner of the election.

One night's debate is not going to change voter opinions on the key issues. Nor will it change the basic bias of issues like crime,

taxes, and defense toward Republicans or that of education, the elderly, and the environment toward Democrats. Even if you "defeat"
your opponent on his issues, he'll win because *his* issues will be rati-
fied as *the* issues of the campaign.

You may have persuaded the voters who watched that night
that you are as tough as your opponent is on crime, but if you are a
Democrat and your opponent is a Republican, the crime issue is going
to work for him regardless of one night's debate. If the debate was
about crime, then crime is *the* issue and if crime is *the* issue, you'll lose.
But if you succeeded, as a Democrat, in making the debate more about
education than about crime, the odds are you will gain the edge even
if your adversary argued well on the education issue.

The trick is to make sure that *your* content and *your* issues
predominate. That's tough to do when reporters are asking the questions. They have the power to take the debate where they want. Most
debates allow for follow-up questions where reporters can complain
if the candidates don't prove responsive to their questions. So a candidate can't just ignore what the reporter asks. Instead, he must practice giving short and crisp answers so that he can use the balance of
his answering time to talk about what he really wants to talk about—
his issues.

A reporter might ask a Democrat, "Why did you vote to raise
taxes sixty times in the state legislature?" His answer might be, "You
know that most of those votes were unanimous and were for minor
increases in fees so that the users of the service paid for it, and the
taxpayers didn't have to kick in. But sometimes budget issues concern
education. As you know, I've always been a strong supporter of programs for our children. . . ." Now, the candidate is free to fill the balance of his time talking about his issue—education.

In this struggle to dominate the content and subject matter of
the debate, attacks on one's opponent serve not merely to besmirch

him, but to distract him from talking about his own issues and force him to address your candidate's concerns instead. Even if every one of candidate A's attacks on candidate B are fully rebutted and factually answered, if B uses all his time answering A's attacks, he will have lost the chance to inject his own issues into the debate. The counter, of course, is to answer attacks in the shortest possible time, allowing the candidate under attack to spend most of his time limit talking about his affirmative issues.

Want to know who won a debate? Don't listen to the pundits. Just add up the number of minutes spent on each issue by the two candidates combined and figure out if the issue favors the Democrat or the Republican. If a Democrat spent ten minutes talking about education and ten talking about taxes, but the Republican talked about schools for only two minutes and devoted fifteen minutes of his time to discussing taxes, a total of twelve minutes would have been spent on education and twenty-five on taxes. Education is a Democratic issue and taxes are a Republican issue, so the advantage in this debate would go to the Republican.

The image part of a debate is overrated. Sometimes, a candidate looks or sounds awful: Nixon in 1960, Carter in 1980, or Reagan in the first debate of 1984. But the vast majority of debates show little that is new about either candidate's style. An embarrassing moment can sometimes cast a pall over a debate—Ford's refusal to admit that the nations of Eastern Europe were Soviet satellites in 1976; Bentsen's "you are no Jack Kennedy" line in the vice presidential debate of 1988; or Dukakis's lame answer on the death penalty in 1988—but again, these instances are rare. Most debates are won or lost based on the issue content of the clash, not on the charisma of the candidates.

CHAPTER 44

What Is Momentum?

G EORGE BUSH CALLED IT "the big Mo" after his pace-setting defeat of Bob Dole in the 1988 New Hampshire Republican Primary.

Momentum. What is it?

In football games, it is the increased adrenaline flow, fan support, motivation, and desire brought about by a touchdown on offense or an interception on defense. In politics, it is the increase in donations, voter awareness, news coverage, and receptivity to advertising caused by an unexpected win or a stronger-than-anticipated finish.

The key words here are "unexpected" and "stronger than anticipated." We are the worst enemies of our own momentum. As candidates, staff, and consultants swell with pride and ego as the surge of victory approaches, we talk and we talk and we talk. Our talk, the natural emission of grandiosity within, kills our momentum. It makes the unexpected, expected; the stronger-than-anticipated, the anticipated.

In the 1976 presidential race of Senator Birch Bayh of Indiana for the Democratic nomination, everybody knew that Jimmy

Carter was the front-runner. Most people felt that liberal Arizona congressman Mo Udall was his main challenger. Behind these two ran a pack of candidates that included Washington Senator Henry Jackson, Oklahoma Senator Fred Harris, and Birch Bayh.

One day, Bayh's tracking polls showed that he had taken second place in New Hampshire on the heels of an exceptionally strong showing in the Iowa caucuses. From an also-ran, Bayh's people now saw their candidate in contention—the putative "alternative to Carter." Sugar plums danced before their eyes. From here, they imagined that Bayh's magnetic personality and warm smile would defeat Carter's personality and smile. They saw how they could win the nomination. From there, they could see him defeating Gerry Ford in the November election. From there . . .

Alas, they talked and talked and talked. The press heard them. It published a prediction that Bayh would finish in second place in New Hampshire. But it was not to be. Bayh fell just slightly short of Udall and finished a close third, well above the other candidates. Bayh's finish was a very strong one—light-years ahead of the also-ran status he had been assigned. On its face, it looked like a three-way race for the nomination.

But Bayh's staff had talked too much. Their talk of finishing second finished them. Now they had finished third, so the results were not "better than anticipated" but "worse than anticipated." It was a "blow," not a "boost," in the eyes and words of the press. Bayh's goose was cooked. His people had cooked it by blabbing.

The lesson: Momentum is one part victory combined with one part secrecy and one part bluff. You have to let the press dump on you, deride your chances, say you're finished, and call you "history" to be able to capture momentum when you confound their predictions. It's a little like hazing to enter a college fraternity. You have to pay your dues.

Then, when you come out "better than anticipated," you have to let the press discover you and publicize that you now have "momentum." Donors, voters, politicians, and more importantly, other reporters read the stories and presto: momentum.

Then, fasten your seat belts and keep your wits about you. It's a heady ride.

The Uses of Defeat

IN POLITICS, neither victory nor defeat is all it's made up to be. Some defeats resemble Carthage, where the Romans burned and sacked the city and then plowed salt into the soil so it would never rise again. Other defeats are only temporary. The loser can recover and fight again another day.

Candidates look to the day of the election as the end of the process. True professionals realize it's just a way station. The real questions remain after election day the same as they were before: What are your vital signs? What is your name recognition? Your favorability? Your vote share? After all, the electorate isn't going anywhere; they'll stay in the district until the next election day. If you came through defeat with a high vote share, though short of a majority, with good recognition and acceptable favorability, you've only lost a battle, not the war.

On the other hand, there's Carthage. When your image has been scorched with effective and unanswered negative ads, and the other side has plowed salt into your soil by driving your favorability to hell and back, it's time to think about selling insurance for a living.

In many states, the electorate just doesn't like to elect you the first time out. They want to see you come back the next time, having taken your licking. Pennsylvania is like that. In 1978, Bob Casey lost his race for governor. He lost again in 1982 and came back to win in 1986. Why do states torment their candidates so? Sometimes, they want to get to know you over many years before they'll let you win. Perhaps voters like chastened and humiliated candidates—they make more tractable governors. Or maybe they just get tired of watching you die.

In many congressional districts, losing is an integral part of winning the next time out. Familiarity and intimacy between the candidate and the voter is a key part of the equation in the election of a congressman. Unlike a senator or governor, voters see their local representative as more like their personal advocate in the distant dome of Congress. In many House races, they won't kiss on the first date. Remember: Newt Gingrich lost twice before he was elected to Congress—both in the same district.

So how do you fall so you can get up again?

The more positive your campaign, the better your chances of not wearing out your welcome. Scorched-earth campaigns alienate everybody who doesn't vote for you and a lot of the people who do. Negative ads trigger negatives back—negatives that don't do your credibility or your favorability any good. But positive, issue-oriented commercials that spell out the differences you have with your adversary in respectful, objective terms only serve to build your reputation for the next time out.

Sometimes, it's a good idea to challenge an unbeatable but aging incumbent so that you can move into the on-deck circle to succeed him when he retires. In fact, there is nothing to make an elected official of long tenure and advanced age look forward to the Florida sunshine more than a tough reelection race every two years.

The key variable in recovering from a defeat is whether you see the district or the state as a long-term investment to be nurtured and developed, as a quick opportunity for a speculative gain through an opportunistic win. If you care about your base, develop your image, and network carefully, it will last until the next election.

What should you do after you lose?

Nurture your donors. Grow closer to them. Find more of them. Act like you won. Stay in the district. Service your constituents—even if they aren't yours yet. Stay involved in community issues. Get your face in the paper a lot. Find a position that allows you to remain visible. Study the returns and figure out where you need work. Spend a lot of time in the areas you lost so that you can come back.

Take your defeat gracefully and cheerfully. Be a good sport. Smile even though it hurts.

⌐ EPILOGUE ⌐

The Future

The issues will be new. Not because the year begins with a "2" as opposed to a "1," but because the dawn of the millennium comes at a time of an unusual winding-down of issues that have dominated our domestic and foreign agendas for half a century or more.

CHAPTER 46

The Issues of the First Years of the Twenty-First Century

I N THE LAST YEARS of the twentieth century, the key issues that have dominated our global politics have come to closure. Communism is dying. Global democracy is on the rise. On the domestic front, the budget is balanced, crime is dropping, welfare rolls have dropped by half. The key questions that have polarized our process in the past decades are fading from view as we enter a new century, a new millenium. What will be the issues of the future?

The environment will likely loom very large. If warnings of global warming and ozone depletion are correct, the environment must become one of our key issues. If the low-lying areas of our planet will indeed be flooded, displacing hundreds of millions of people, and if we are to be exposed to ever more carcinogenic emissions from the sun, the environmental issue will obviously dominate our politics. As disaster scenes of tornadoes, forest fires, mudslides, fierce hurricanes, and earthquakes proliferate on the nightly news, climate change is likely to rise to the top of our national agenda. Yet, these events are trivial compared to the major dislocations that true environmental catastrophe would trigger. When rain falls in the wrong place and tra-ditionally arable areas become parched and dry, global images of famine will come to galvanize public opinion even further.

Just as the nuclear issue forced a global effort to avoid another world war and brought about a balance that largely preserved the peace, the environmental issue may well catalyze efforts to subordi-nate economic self-interest to a planetary consciousness. If the nuclear issue and the resultant superpower competition led to a global system of diplomacy and conflict management, the environmental issue will likely bring about a worldwide network of economic coordination and environmental regulation. In all likelihood, the environment will be a key issue of the next twenty years.

Just as the physics of Einstein, Fermi, and Oppenheimer laid the basis for the political issues of the last half of the twentieth cen-tury, it is likely that the Genome Project, the decoding of human DNA, will usher in a host of political issues in the next century. We are very close to seeing the last generation of human beings born in a natural, unaltered state. Genetic engineering, first to block heredi-tary diseases and later to alter personality and intelligence, will likely create a new race of humans during the course of the next century.

The political implications of this scientific capacity are stag-gering. The current debate about cloning misses the point entirely. Cloning is the opposite of evolution—it is a freezing of evolution by the exact recreation of a preexisting human being. It is, rather, the cre-ation of new people with new abilities, life spans, and capabilities that must concern us. The old question of when the computer would out-think man is obsolete. The issue now is whether we are about to cre-ate a new man, endowed with capacities that dwarf our own.

I believe that such change, as Teilhard de Chardin points to in his *Phenomenon of Man,* is akin to "seizing the tiller of the world" by taking evolution into our own hands. I think that it is both inevitable and highly desirable. But its potential for misapplication is so substantial that it cannot fail to be one of the core issues of our political future.

Finally, if we are blessed with continued prosperity and real income growth within our nation, the generosity and ecumenical spirituality of the American people will increasingly lead toward a demand for America to play a greater global role in fighting poverty and helping people in the third world. Foreign aid has a bad name because the governments to which it goes have bad names. But while foreign assistance falls into greater disrepute, American charitable contributions have shot up in the 1990s, far outpacing the modest level increases in the equally prosperous 1980s. We are becoming a nation of philanthropists. Increasingly, the human suffering in Africa, Asia, and Latin America will concern the American people and become an important factor in our domestic politics.

Whether these speculations are accurate or not, one thing is certain. The issues of the twentieth century are largely over. Through two world wars and a cold war, we have arrived at an international consensus built around free-market democracies and human rights that is not likely to be altered. Domestically, the deficit is a thing of the past and the reductions in welfare and crime seem likely to last. The conservative challenge to the liberal idea of expansive government has led to a division of roles between the government and the marketplace that is unlikely to be relitigated successfully.

This period of consensus will be succeeded by one of polarization as the new issues of the twenty-first century call for different solutions from different ends of the political spectrum, and democracy works at what it is best at—solving the problems of our future.

CHAPTER 47

The Politics of the Future: A Peek at the Brave New World of Internet Democracy

THE MOVEMENT AWAY from representative democracy and toward direct control of public policy by voters is bound to accelerate as new technology and wider public familiarity with the Internet overcomes the logistical barriers to holding national town meetings. The politics of the future will be shaped by referenda in which voters directly indicate their policy choices. With fifty-four million Americans using the Internet, the day of the national town meeting is not far off. With more Internet users, such a forum is almost inevitable.

Here's how it will likely work.

Private entrepreneurs will establish a Web site for a national town meeting. They will widely publicize its existence and sponsor referenda in which people will vote by logging on to the site. As more voters register their opinions, the media will take increasing notice. Within a few years, the Web-site town meetings will attract tens of millions of voters on each referendum. As the usage swells, so will the national attention to these votes.

Eventually, virtually every issue of any import considered in Congress will also be posted for voter participation on the Web site. When the House or Senate votes on Fast Track for trade agreements, for example, the national town meeting will take up the topic. Television and radio talk shows will likely hold discussions and debates on the issue. Interest groups will seek to shape public opinion by advertising. Newspapers will run specials on the question. All attention will be focused on the Web-site referendum.

On the day of the town meeting, tens and tens of millions of people will log on to the Internet, access the town-meeting Web site, and cast their ballots. The next day the results will be posted on the Web and likely broadcast through the media. Congressmen will anxiously pore through the results to figure out how their district voted.

Will members of Congress be influenced by the town-meeting result? You bet. It will have an impact far, far greater than a poll. In a survey, a congressman can learn how his constituents feel about a given issue. He can follow their advice or reject it and hope that the issue won't bite him on election day. But he dares not ignore a voter referendum where his constituents know they have participated and registered their views, know the outcome of the referendum, and can examine how their congressman finally votes.

If hundreds of thousands of people in a congressional district have indicated their preference for defeat of Fast Track legislation, the congressman who represents them will, in all likelihood, meekly follow their guidance. Were he to ignore a poll, he would suffer because voters didn't agree with his position. But if he ignores a town-meeting Internet referendum, he will also have to explain why he didn't listen to the will of the people of his district, which was so clearly manifest in the Web-site balloting.

As the power of the Web-site referenda becomes more apparent, media coverage of national town meetings will intensify. Eventually, these votes will become national dramas, anxiously followed by the political establishment. While Congress is not about to cede its power by permitting the same kind of referenda and initiatives permitted in California, national town meetings will become their de facto equivalent.

We are about to enter an era of pure Jeffersonian democracy, where Internet town meetings will convey daily or weekly advice to elected officials and structure most of the major decisions on important issues. In such an environment, our elected representatives will experience the same drop in power that the state legislators of California have already had to live through. In that state, most important issues are decided directly by voters, not by their legislators. Nationally, the Web site town meeting will dominate our politics in the future.